AF480243

# Through the Grapevine I Heard

Inquiries and Book Orders should be addressed to:

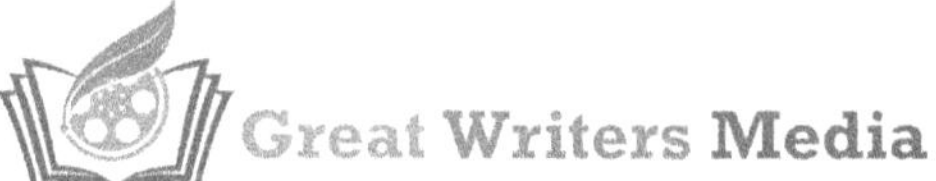

Great Writers Media
Email: info@greatwritersmedia.com
Phone: 877-556-0487

ISBN: 979-8-89175-063-0 (sc)
ISBN: 979-8-89175-064-7 (hc)
ISBN: 979-8-89175-062-3 (ebk)

# A Face without a Name

A face without a name
A smile to bare
It erases all the pain
A face without a name
Childhood poverty
Hard working slave labor
Things don't seem to change
A face without a name
A silent prayer a ray of hope
Somebody please hear me
For my cries is rapidly
My pain is invisible
A brighter and better tomorrow
Drift slowly down the slope
Bring mercury to me
A face without a name
God let me not
Drown in my own sorrow
A face without a name
How long will life burden me?
The shock of life pain
Rich man money
Poor man knowledge
Walking between two worlds
Is there anything to gain?
An almost forgotten promise
Shatter vision remain the same
A face without a name

# A Walk on the Beach

I'm going down to the beach
I will look out across the sea
I see an imaginary vaguer
Coming toward me
The water will renew my mind
The water will cleanse my feet
Seashells and seaweeds
Clams and pearls I'm hoping
I'll find
Build a castle out of sand
Who knows who you will meet?
A blonde girl a handsome man
A walk on the beach
I will stay until
Calm falling moon go down
The happy rising sun comes up
High tides low waves
A surfer dream
On a hot sunny day
The eastern stars all around
A long walk on the beach
A seagull baby like cry
The watchful life guard
They must have six eyes
A walk down on the beach
Picnics and volley ball
Little boys walking their dogs
A walk on the beach
Enjoy your summer fun
The season is rotating
Shortly it will be fall again

The hot days will be done
A walk down on the beach
Laugh and be happy
Leave your prints
In the wet sand of your feet
A long walk on the beach

# A Home Garden of Love

A home is where the heart is
Full with love, and so much joy
Memories of the moment
A pair of caring arms to embrace
A lasting touch
The moment so special, it'll never go to waste
A home garden of love
A very special place
From the beginning to the ending
It'll leave a smile upon your face
There are red and yellow roses
Four o'clock that sing and rock
Elephant ear plants spring up so high
Tulips and Lilies
Gardenias to smell with our noses
Home is where our heart is
A beautiful garden that grows
To replenish and nourish our bodies
With the minerals from the earth
It makes our souls glow
From our heads down to our toes
A wooden bench perched
Beneath the weeping willow tree
Hummingbirds flying all around
The canaries are singing, as sweet as can be
There are vegetables of all kind
Potatoes, squashes, and running beans
Fruit trees a plenty
We have cherry, apple, fig, and grape
The children loves to pick them
My!
There are so many
A home garden of love

# Acceptance

Dear God,

I don't remember choosing
A stern mother
I don't remember choosing
A farmer father
I don't recall
All the family members
That I was assigned to
In this lifetime
I accept all the things
That I can't change about them
I will love them
I can also choose to
Walk away from them
I devoted and rerouted
My time, my energy
In changing me

# African Heritage or Rumor

Have you heard the myth?
All Africans are dizzy. Africans don't how to read or write.
Yes, the Europeans taught Africans their skills. Africans has no expectations.
Who labels history as this lie?
From our motherland came kings and queens.
Our motherland spit out the finest warriors. As history unfolds our kings and queens wouldn't be happy.
Down with the Dahome yes and other tribes.
Africa would mean land of the slaves. Africa is the gateway of knowledge.
Before paper or books, black man discovers skills.
Who are they to label Africa as green.
Yes, green only in the farm land.
Chained and bonded we were robbed of our pride, stripped of dignity.
No more chains, no whips only hands and hard work.

As history is told Africa is the mother of self-confidence. If man can take away the African heritage then it's him who is green.
History should be known for its black sisters and brother about our motherland.
Land where our past kings and queen slayed up on.
Land where our mothers gave birth to her babies
Land where no Europeans can ever claim they taught us.
Africans yes Africa let your light shine.

From this mother land which I came.
From this land one day I shall return.
Full of pride
Full of skills.

# Ain't No Gold

Ain't no gold in them cotton fields
No gold
In them cotton fields
Only tears of yester years
Trails of blood of my ancestors
In prints
Trying to walk for freedom
Bleeding of the past
As they kneeled
Ain't no gold
In them cotton fields
The bloody
Sweaty
Bitter
Hated
Tearful truth
Slicing the future heels
No gold
No gold
In them cotton fields

# All Dogs Don't Have Tales

What?
All dogs don't have tales
If it walks like a dog
If it barks like a dog
Then dog gone it
It is a dog
They don't discriminate
Some are females
They come in all colors and sizes.
If a dog says I love you
Should you believe it?
Rest assure a dog
Always have a second house
That is right
Don't blame me
For your mistrust
Don't blame me
For your insecurity
Your lies and devilish ways
Will catch you
And pile that nasty
Puppy food on your plate
The plate in which you
Push on someone else table
Some of the old dogs
Are worse than the young one
A dog wags it's tail
Shiver below the knees
And lie like a dog
I was told every dog has their day
Well rest assure
Every puppy has their night.

It makes me laugh
When some people
Think they are larger than life
The same God that created you
Also made me to
Yes, assure you will
Get just what is coming to you
Trust me all dogs don't have tales

# Aint Nobody Crying Over You

Who do you think you are
I guess you must be
That special star that fell from the sky
I guess you must be
That wet teardrop
From a crying lady eye
I guess you must be
The twinkle in a star
That ray from the sun
You must be
That finally yes when everything is said and done
But baby
Ain't nobody crying over you

# An Overdose of God

The bible said, treat people the way you want to be treated
The bible also said you got to reap what you sowed
It's called karma
When you stop lying
Stop plotting
Stop scheming
Stop trying to hurt other people
Stop all your evil ways
Stop trying to destroy other good blessing
Stop trying to block someone else progress
God got your name
God got your number
Your phone is on speed dial
God know where you live at
You will harvest what you planted
So deal with it

# Antsy Pants

Slow down
You're moving too fast
There are roses outside
Stop to smell them
There are birds
Chirping in the trees
Insects that sting
Flies that light up
At night
Rushing into the unknown
Who know what it will bring
Breathe
Count to ten
Exhale
Push the stale air out
Sweetheart
There's a whole big
Wide world
Waiting for you
Too explore
You can't get
From London
Or France
By missing all
The important details
The road map
Shows step by steps
All of the green lights

The red lights
The flashing caution lights
Stop
Go
Right
Left
Signs
Just slow down
Then follow
The instructions
Antsy pants

# At the Crack of Dawn

At the crack of dawn
The sun hasn't rose
A blue orange paint
The peeking poking
Of a shadow of light
It looks very faint
The beautiful sky
Will bring light to us all
As the sun
Highlight the sky
Just before
The crack of dawn

# Dear B.T.

You can never talk about me. The side hustles I learned it here. From you.
The Peter Pan fly out of your body experiences, I learned them from you right here.
How to walk with a swagger, how to talk like butter. Smooth but sweet, with a side of grade
A honey
I spy, fly, up on the walls.
The chants, the rhythms, the dances. I learned it from you.
You can never call me a liar.
You can never call me a pimp
You can never call me whore
A bitch
A witch
A Itch
Someone unfit
A trifling heifer
A Thief
None of that bad stuff
I was just as green as grass
I learned it all from you

# Bama Girl

Hee haw
How y'all doing
Bama girl
All the way
Hopscotch
Tic tac toe
Baseball
Basketball
Catching lightning bugs
Butterflies
Apple trees
Pear trees
Fig trees
Yellow jacks
Wasps
Big black bumble bees
I am a Bama girl
Cornrows
Square dance
Football
Soccer
Band practice
Stepping
Saxophone
Flute blowing
Tumble flips
Cheerleaders getting a swirl and lift

The bulldog mascot
We can't be beat
Our school fundraiser
Sell that candy
Get the pot going
A quick fish fry
We all stand together
United by colors
Sticking together
Sailing very high too
That old white and blue
Until we die.

# Being Bad

How much fun can it be
I never got a chance
You see
Good!
Good!
Good!
Was what I had to be
I would love to be in a movie
To express
The trap up energy
Bottled up inside
The bad role
That is the bitch
I want to take
Her out for a drive
I know I can channel her
Very well
Cruella Devil
Cinderella stepmother
Cybill Shepherd
Watch out now
Some hot attitude
Turning like a ferry wheel
I want a role
Utilize this for one
Being Bad
I see the good side
So much fun
I can have

# Bitter husband ex-wife

Bitter husband
Unhappy ex-wife
When I met you
You had so many hidden secrets
You had a closet full of demons
A graveyard of skeletons
You had a hidden agenda
A clever smile outside
But a sour heart on the inside
You let me walked into
A spiritual ass whopping ambush
I didn't see these demons coming
You had haters that hated me
A hater that hated my kids
I was the feline with almost a half of litter
In their eyes;
I was never good enough for you
You had a choice to love me or hate
You meet me with hate
You had your part in running me away
You can stay out there with your hate
Keep all your devilment
Pure hate spells
Pure bottle spells
Pure death spells
Hiding your hands
While wearing God on your sleeves
I forgave you for
All that dirt you did to me
This karma got to be paid
Don't call me
I meant just what I said
I don't want to be bothered
With none of your asses

Some people was put on earth
Not for the good of others
Please leave me alone
You made your choice
You deal with this
You calling me sad
I didn't cause your sadness
I wish you love
I wish you joy
I wish peace to everybody
But you never wish that for us
There were so many lies
Spread about me
I was this
I was that
I was angry and spread malice on people
I don't know anybody
Worth my time or money
Y'all is talking about yourself
All that dirt y'all did to people
It was always my name being drag through the mud
Rumors and made up lies
I slept around
That my ex-husband caught me cheating
In the bed with another man
I got a new flash for you
I don't go around sleeping with other people
I made a vow before God
I made a vow before man
Then turn around and diss God like that.
I was faithful to someone who didn't deserve it
Your friends in the neighborhood
Was talking about you
Your extra marital affairs
Asking me if all that stuff
About you is true
You're grown

I couldn't make you stay
You couldn't wait until the ink dry
On the divorce paper
I hope you found what you where looking for
Before you hug your prize possession
Did you get your time worth
Did you get your money worth
Most of your life
You were controled by someone else
You're not around anymore
I don't have a mother
Go on with that control shit
Wade over yonder
These trifling daughters of a man
Still trying to stir up shit
Bitches be gone
I am not going to call nobody
I meant nobody
I don't give a shit about it.
You didn't love me when I met you
You show in the hell
Don't love me now
The End!

# Burger King

I see Burger King
It's in my back yard
Just cross the grass
Pass the trees
It's so close
There are two
Little girls
That I know
They work there
Making that extra change
For school
Preparing up
Looking pretty
Going out to eat
Chowing down
As they sit in their seats
The darkness set in
I see two little girls
Walking through the trees
Coming home
From a late night work
My eyes watch them
Just like a hawk
Making sure they're safe
Now it's just one little girl
Coming home from work
This little girl
Don't have a care in this world
Throwing caution to the wind
Walking home so late at night
If you need me
Scream

Through the rain
Through the snow
Going to work
Bundle up and off she go
At her job
Out the back door
Across the grass
Walking pass the trees
To Burger King
Be careful
Be safe
Check your surrounding
Keep a happy smile
On your face
At your job
T and L
That's what make
The day go by fast
Good tips
I know you will last

# Changing Seasons

The seasons may come
And the seasons may go
In and out
As do the passing minute of time
Life and death
The cold blistering winter
Blooming beautiful spring
Hot roasting wet summer
Mild calm dry autumn
Everything living inhale air upon the earth
Not one beautiful leaf is left
Life and then rebirth
Living and then death
In and out of seasons
Upon God green earth
Planting and plucking
Minute after minute
Cutting and pruning
We all have a purpose in life
Right down to the reason
In and out of this changing season

# Caught Up

Caught up in the moment
I don't understand
Too young to understand
Just what the eyes are viewing
The mind is turning
Trying to process
The great big picture
How long
Do
Long last
Caught up in the moment
The friends
The family
That I use too have
Time changed
Things changed
Earthly and spiritually
Processing what the mind see
Drawing a line through
That which was not
Meant to be
A flight up
A right so very up
A process
Man that's a hike

# Childhood Flashback

How I long
To go home
Back deep in them woods
Big black old wash pot
Some maple wood
Some dry old planks
Everybody gathering at the school
I hear children laughing
The crowd travel from all over
It's called May Day
Hotdogs
Hamburgers
White light bread
An ice can of soda
Ketchup
Pickles
Mustard
I can smell the grease getting hot
They are having a fish fry
Black pepper flying through the air
The warming of the evening sun
Young people
Old people
We're having so much fun
So much fun!
No trouble
Everybody is enjoying themselves
School competition to plait
The May pole
We're going to beat them
We always do
Sorry Alberta

Decked out in yellow, and blue
Those are the colors
Of the mascot
The B-Eagles
A pair of blue jeans
A brand-new white t-shirt
Everybody is wearing that
Hey that will work
The principal sitting in her office over looking
The school event
Sellers sitting beneath their tents
The sun is going down
The crowd moving away
What a day
This was in May

# Childhood Love

I know my ancestors love me
Most are dead
On a spiritual plane
I know they visit me
I can feel their present
My aunt is eighty-four years old
Auntie N
Uncle B; aka Uncle B-wife
Auntie N calls me every year and say happy birthday
Auntie N even sing happy birthday to me
I am sorry my ancestor believed in me, when I didn't believe in myself
They have eyes to see far beyond the sight of a child
The wisdom of Solomon

# Cinderella

Cinderella step sisters
Was three crystal clear triple bitches
They moan
They groan
They couldn't get along
They made her scrub
They made her rub
They made her carry the water
Cook all the food
Did all the sewing of clothes
They were so mean to her
They were a triple crystal clear bitches
The end.

# Computer Teacher

*Question:* I wonder why this teacher is working us so hard?

*Answer:* I believe student come to learn how to learn. After learning to use the computer, they will find more self-confidence.

*Question:* Will we ever need this hand cramping mind-boggling stuff?

*Answer:* Probably not. The hand cramping is going the way of the horse and buggy. But the confidence that come from learning to take control of a horse and buggy, make what follow easy as pie.

*Question:* I wonder if this teacher will ever remember a name or a face?

*Answer:* Yes. Teachers devote their lives to their students. I have no other career than helping students believe in themselves.

*Question:* Is Mr. Singer giving us this work to help or just being mean?

*Answer:* the work you do satisfy your need to prove yourself and it satisfies my need to feel productive too.

*Question* What would my grade be?

*Answer:* an A you get from a class whatever you put into it. It's my job to see you give your best effort.

Mr. Singer thank you for seeing beyond our point and given us what we needed instead of what we wanted. That's a lot of desktop publishing.

Click, click and click
Drag pull give it a tick
I'm flying through desktop
Write a poem or watch the girls shop
I can create bulletins and flyers
Send a telegram to a good homebuyer
O'how desktop opens my world
I'm flowing like a priceless pearl
I'll give credit where credit is due.
Thank to my computer teacher Mr. Singer
My uncertainty and fears are gone
Me and my computer on a throne
I'm happy I took this course
Learning understanding that's my source
Mr. Singer your work and teaching is not in vain
Edit spellcheck print it that's my game
Click, click, and click

In my memory forever will it stick

# Control With No Control

What's control
How do you control
What is the goal of your capture
Do you plan to wreak havoc
Do you plan to release
Easy now
Don't take control of another soul for too long
Some human beings tend to hold resentment
Some people tend to hold grudges
Some people will down right committee the unthinkable
Don't take control over a person over the age of eighteen
With the right frame of mind and the ability
To make good sound judgment
It's not easy
I say release
Release
Let go
Too much control
Is a bad thing
Some people want to be free
Some people want others dictating their lives
Give your kids space to live and be a kid
Give your husbands space to be a man
Give your wife space to be a woman
Let them breathe

Don't take control so much
Don't make it that choking kind
Too much bondage is not good for the spirit
Too much control is a path of pure destruction
Control some
But don't take control forever
Release
Release
Breathe
Let go

# Cotton Candy Door

Cotton candy door
Big wide and deep
Once you enter no return
Cotton candy shore
So soft so sweet
Sweeter than honey suckers
On a warm June day
Cotton candy door
The bees buzz for more
Sweeter than juice of
A ripe good fruit
So tender and plumb
Cotton candy door
Take what you please
Not without permission
A token of giving
Cotton candy door
The way sales lady makes a living
Cotton candy sells more and more
Cotton candy an open door
Next time around
A new set of bees flying for more
When will you close your candy store?

The tile of this poem is called cremation and I hope you enjoy reading it.

I have search high and I have search low, I don't who I was reincarnated with but I feel very strongly about being cremated when my life is all over.

That is my decision and no one can change how I feel each man and woman is entitled to his or her opinion and choice.

Unless the earth plain was ready for a ghost or horrible and terrible things. That right ashes to ashes and dust to dust. From the dust man was made from the dust shall he return once again. This poem is for all the people who agree with me and those who support my theory.

## Cremation

Don't lay
My honors in the dust.
That way my soul
Will not crumble
Nor will it rust
From the dust I came
Back to ashes once again
Don't lay
My honor in the dust
Forever in God
Will my spirit trust
Burn my lifeless bones
It's all over I'm gone
I have paid my tithes
My soul want to move on
Don't weep nor groan
In the spirit world
I have travel on
Don't lay
My honor in the dust
At least my soul
Will not crumble nor rust

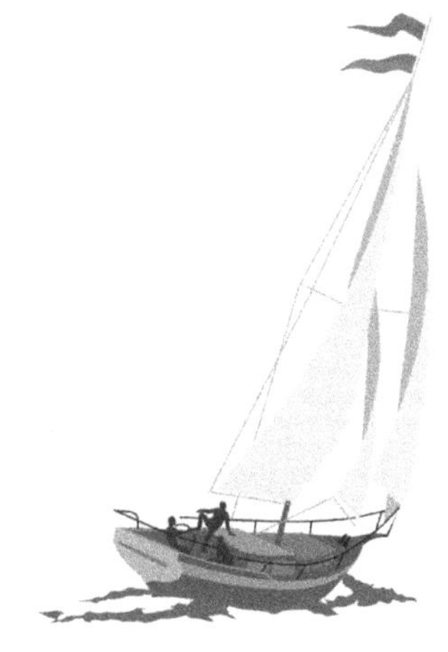

# Date

I had a date
He pick me up
He was driving
He smile at me
He ask me
How're you doing?
I smile and said fine
I asked
Where are we going?
He replied
I am taking you
Down memory lane

# Dear Daddy:

The ghost of yesterday PART II

I am sorry daddy the ghost has came home to haunt. There's a saying chicken, has come home to roost.

A chicken is a living breathing thing. A ghost can move freely, go wherever it wants to. A ghost can linger around and sometimes never seem to die in spirit. The ghosts has return to haunt. I am sorry daddy please forgive me. The best gift anyone can give is the gift of forgiveness. When I was younger I was coached to sneak and tiptoe and steal all the loose change out of your pockets.

Tiptoe and very quiet about it. I felt so guilty about it. I almost squeal like a pig, a fright one too. Daddy the act of deeds will catch up with you. No deeds go unpunished, if good then good, if bad then the scales must be balanced.

In life you learn lessons every day. One thing I know for sure justice nor karma has a time line. It caught up with me. My close flesh is retuning my balance of karma to me.

The same bad deeds were laid upon my tables to eat.

Daddy, I am sorry. Perhaps you need those few dollars to get a soda or buy some cigarettes paper or tobacco. You know the one in the red can called Prince Albert. Some gas for the car sound good also.

Well something is not worth the time and effort.

Daddy, don't be mad at me. For I am sure you have stood before God in the spirit world and have a clean slate. Other than that, besides cutting the light off as my two little sisters and I was watching the M.T.V show that late Saturday night. You yelled "Go to bed and cut that t.v. off".

We decided to test you, I heard foot steps down the hallway. Quick with the eyes I saw that belt that was in your hands.

So I jumped up grab the string to the light switch you couldn't see.

All I heard was stumbling everywhere.

I felt was bad

Once I found out you was alright. We all laugh, and laugh out loud.

Janet Jackson was dancing and singing. It was a rhythm nation. I was trying to learn some new dance moves.

Well no one got a spanking that night.
Sorry daddy M.T.V on came on, only during the weekend.

Forgive me, I love you
Y.O.D.

# Dear Friend (Frenemy)

Dear Frenemy:

It gives me a great pleasure to get this cargo of my shoulders and out of my system.
I tell you.
Wow you're a unique piece of work.
I must omit.
You stole the cake when it comes to selfishness
I can't believe you're a big grown ass adult and wants to blame me for your problems.
Well guess what?
I will not take the blame for your mistakes.
Not at all. Nope no way
You're very selfish. The only time you know me is when you want to use me to your benefits.
When you need a favor
What kind of fool do you think I am?
What kind of fool do I look like to you
A crazy one
A dumb blonde one
A green one
God is not going to handcuff me, and take me to court. For all the trials and errors that you made.
I didn't steal your money, I had absolutely nothing to do with that.
Sorry it happened to you.
Find the person whom you gave it to, and fight with them.
I can recognize game, I can smell bullshit five hundred miles away.
I did finish school but you think I graduated from a stupid school ok.
I beg you to borrow some money and you would let me have not one red penny.
Boy did that hurt.
What a low blow.
God made sure I was taken care of.
I got money in the mail, for a contest I entered, I picked up pennies and turn them in.
I used to turn my nose up, if I saw a penny on the ground.
The yester years living in Boston, walking on by all the pennies laying on the ground.
What a difference a day makes.

I paid of my purchase and I will survive. I have to get rid of the hurt lurking inside my solar plexus cabinet.

It's not good at all

You open my eyes up wide. It was revealing what type of person you really are. I was warned, well guess what lesson learned.

Yes God I got it; lesson learned.

I refuse to be blamed for your troubles your mistakes that you and your lover made.

I close this letter to say.

I send you the white light of love, peace and blessing.

I am moving on and will not be looking back.

I pray one day you'll stop lying, stealing, and scheming people.

The joker even get played at his own game.

Peace.

# Dear Neighbor

Dear Neighbor:

I don't mean to be rude.
I am
Who I am
It's plain to see
I am still struggling with childhood trauma.
I am trying to work through these struggles
A very dark; light side rotating in my mind
It's like Doctor Jekyll and Mr. Hyde
I got my own Pandora's box
I hide it real well
The creepy side of this secret
Sometimes consume me
You make think I am mean
No offense
I don't care what you think
I haven't thought a minutes and one second about you!
I have never complain about you
Or your wild dog
The drunks; weed smoking
Throat choking ass company you be keeping
Never ever complain
I just don't give a cold shit about y'all
When I wake up in the morning
It's me and God
I give glory and praise to God
I got nothing to say
The first impression is the best one
I have nothing to say
I am struggling with these trauma bonds
Attachment from the past.
Nobody can help me
Nobody
Other than me.

# Dear World

Dear World;


I have never told my daddy I love him, but I showed him that I did. I never told my mamma, that I love her. But deep within my heart I showed her love. I used to help my mamma pick out her clothes. I used to buy my mamma shoes. World don't judge me, for you don't know me.

I learn what I am taught, where we came from. We never stated the words I Love You. We thought if you show it then the world will know it.

I used to buy her little due-hicks to sit around on the ledges of the fireplace.

I never ever disobeyed my mamma. Truly she was a tough, big, beautiful lady. My mamma had that honey brown skin with no wrinkles, and no pimples.

I used to love to style her hair and put her makeup on. I used to wash my mamma hair. I thought mamma was too mean as a teenager, but know looking back down the road, from where I am standing now mamma was the drill sergeant that I needed.

I have never, ever, ever, disrespected my mamma or daddy. NEVER.

A mamma who put order in my life

A mamma who didn't let me go astray

A mamma who taught me how to cook

A mamma who taught me how to wash and clean

How to make and excellent flower garden

The hot topic on pro-life and pro-choice.

Mamma was a woman, who had made mistakes, and I am pretty sure mamma wish there was a choice she could have did different. Well mamma nobody in this world is prefect and sin free. Even thou you got some people who think they're holy than thou.

There is always room for learning and growing. There are two types of learning, the things that you know and leaving room to learn the things in which you don't know.

I sit along and see the ghosts of yesterday, hearing the old recorded conversation play on an invisible tape recorder that don't exist.

# Distance

I'll sleep better
When you're not around
Not dead now
I don't trust you
I need to sleep with both eyes open
What a shame
You think you got love
Just a silly clown
Dragging your heart around
Up
Down
Around
Across the ground and through the mud
What a joke
I keep a tool nearby
Just incase
I have to defend myself
A sleeping man
No not
What a woke man is doing
Nothing wrong
With space
It heal
It repairs
It renews
It reactivates
Timis a sentence
A jail for free
Nothing wrong with it
A moment to think
A peace of heaven
A place where
You can be you
Never be afraid of

Loneliness
Never be
Embarrassed
Embrace it
As a gift
Wrap at your time
Turn it off
Turn it on
As thou
It was a clock

# Double Mirror

I see you in me
A split image
A double mirror
I'm what you picture
Me to be
The good the bad
The ugly the pretty
The dirt the gritty
That devilish smile
That hilarious lie
A natural con artist
Fifty dollars for one try
That slick smooth talk
That crooked little walk
Double mirror
I see you in me
I'm a split image
What else can I be?
I'm that girl with attraction tears
I'm that fifty cent lady
Hustling is my thing
I gotta keeping it real
I see you in me
Black book Madam
Five hundred clients a night
I see you looking at me
A double mirror

Anything for money
Who said I'm wrong
Who said I was right
I see you in the mirror
A split image of me
Question?
How far can an apple
Fall from a tree
A split image of you
Looking at me.

# Drama Queen

Waiting to cause a big scene
A downright natural drama queen
Standing on the front porch
While she light up a cancer torch
Head rag mamma
Minute by minute waiting for drama
Chasing the mailman down
For your welfare check
Shopping, cigarette, and rent you can bet
More broke than a glass vase in a week
This same old ritual you repeat
Change your life drama queen
One hundred miles per hour
On the telephone talking a lot of crap
It's time for your nap
Hit a book, enroll into college
You can get a boatload of understanding and knowledge
Drama queen please
Your welfare is running out
Job training, college registration and expensive childcare
Headaches, midterm, and stress there's no doubt
Stop causing a putrid scene
Change you attitude and life, miss drama queen.

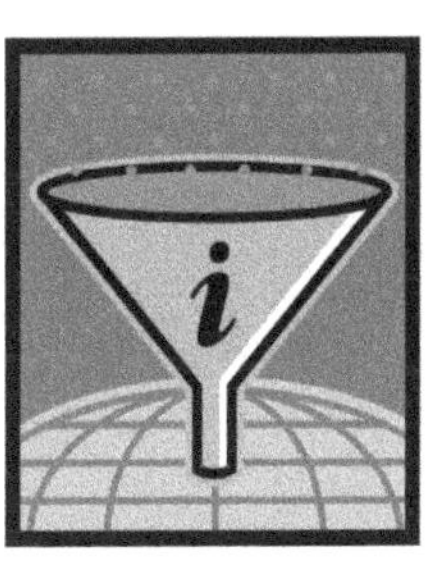

# Due You

So many peeps worry about
Everybody else
Except themselves
What gossip is doing
What liar is doing
Leave old gossip along
Leave old liar along
Everybody problems got you on the run
Mind your own business
Due you
Nobody else can take your place
The road that needs to be travel
The shoes for walking that's your space
Find the road, highway, interstate
That lead to your path
Of happiness
Of peace
Of joy
Due you

# Empty Fridge

The fridge is empty
No food for the children
No food for the family
Living in a world of abundance
Yet someone
Somebody go to bed hungry every day
Every night
Feed the children
Feed the needy
Blessings will surely flow
Flow with fatness
From above
Down below

# Eternal Sleep

Who said sleep is eternal
Is it
Well let me explain
You have people who
Spirits is afraid to journey into the light
Why
So much wrong doing
So very much
God and his angels are waiting
Why run now
You're a spirit
Go ahead and face judgement
Stop hiding
Karma is a rotating wheel
Depend on your life
Big chief in life
Died with so much strife
You can carry karma around
From one cycle to another term
Be mindful how you treat people
Be mindful what you speak about people
Your heart is being judge
Light, or lighter than a feather
Heavy heart
Light heart
You have to reap just what you sow
Every tongue must confess
Every knee shall bow
Think forgiveness
Think of your karma
Not pressing on your chest

# Get Down

Why would it
Benefit me
To get down with you
I see very little comparing
We don't have a lot in common
Yet
You want a drive by quickie
Boy please
You look grimy and sticky
You're not my cup of tea
I don't see the benefits
Of getting down with you
A wet useless night
The swapping of toxic energy
A toxic shock for the soul
Hell to the no
No
No
And then no
I am single
I am very much so happy
No headaches
No heartaches
No sharing dickie wickie
I don't have to gps him
I should know where he at
I just can't imagine
Driving around

Looking for him
Child
Child
Child please
Think twice before
You let anybody
Get down with you
And into your bed

# Food 4 Thoughts

A plate full
Of pettiness
A side order
Of bull shit
Don't give it to me
I don't want
Your mess
I can surely
Live without
The migraines and stress
No need for the pills
No need
For a straight jacket
I got a dose, to make u feel better
If your ass
Is ill
A lump on the head
A foot up your butt
Nothing else
Need to be said
The End

# Goat

Goat the smell
The taste
Goat is a soft cuddly animal.
I prefer to keep them as pets
Not to eat
The smell is musty
Some people make goat soap.
Some people drink goat milk.
I personally don't like the taste. I love goat milk soap.
One of my favorite soap.

# God, Mamma, and Me

Borrow from God
Loan to woman
Born of a woman
Better known as momma
Just a few days ago
Living life like
It may not be a tomorrow
For nobody
Roaming through this college dorm
Called earthplane
Bitter
Sweet
Nasty
Lying
Jealousy
Adultery
Racism
Hatery
Atheist
Baptist
Catholic
Buddhist
Bewitchment
Embezzlement
Bribery
Treachery
Depression
Lesbian
Gays
Bigender
Transgender
Wicca
Hoo-doo
Voo-doo

Santeria
A blood rite
A grimy dirty shame
Throwing dirt on your name
Smearing blood on the ground
In the name of racism
The healer
The killer
You took an Oath
That you would
Serve and Protect
Who and What
The protector became the abuser
Stooping lower than dirt
Just to make yourself look big
Trying to win at all cost
Throwing dirty on mine (our) name
Proceed with cautious
You have a right to remain silent
Anything you do
Anything you say
Will be used against you
Easy with those hurtful words
Easy with those falsified lies
I promise you
It'll hurt you
Before it hurt me
The law of karma
Regifting it back
Ten time fold
The enjoyment of living
The sorrows of dying
Death have never stood at the gates of time
And judge mankind by

Their wealth
The racks of money
The lack of without money
Looks
Color
Sizes
Degrees
Houses
Huts
Cars
Classes
Style
Clubs and Organizations
Death is a time capsule
Waiting to happen to us all
Minute by minute
Time is ticking away
Death don't care about
That material gain
All death wants is your appointed time

# Going to School

Going to school
It was so cool
No police officer to guard the doors
No metal detectors
No fire arm carried
I am not bored anymore
I change schools
I am the P that sit on the hill
Wow wee, wow
So many handsome faces
So many guys
Guys are everywhere
Fresh young
Temporary love is all there
Love sweet love innocent
Five minute in the air
I say it's
Just a puppy love
A fast flare
P the school
That sit on top of the hill
A long bus ride before
The crack of dawn
In the changing seasons
I pray that we make it there
I pray that we make it back
Ernest he is the driver
We're in good hands
A nice brown
Short

But sweet man
He has a voice like a male robin
He can sing
The clouds right out the sky
It's a lot to remember
Going to school
Memories not tape
Filmed
Nor is it erasable
That's what so hot
Was this ever this cool

# Good Night

No light in sight
Darkness cover the dark
Owls are hooting
Crickets are crying
Good night
I see some stars
Up in the sky
Big one
Small stars
Will provide a light
So high in the sky
Everything is so peaceful
So very calm
Good night
Good night
The moon is peeking
Through the clouds
I see a little bit of light

# Got Away

The angels
Must have
Made you
Just for me
But you
Were
The one
That got away
A body
Like
A god
Your lips
Your eyes
Twinkle
Like the stars
I day dream
About us
Holding hands
You laying
In my arms
We're snug than a bug in a rug
Man
man
What a dream
But you were
The one that got away

# Grand Mama Cries

My soul cry out
For your arms
To the woman
Whom I never got to know
I imagine
What you looked like
Invisible tears
Keep me company
Past and presents days
Of me thinking about you
If only
I could have
Embrace your loving arms
If only I could have
Laid my head on
Your gentle warm shoulders
To stare in your eyes
Grand mama
Invisible dreams
Of a child mind
Invisible dreams
Of sweet deep wishes
Of a child
In past time

# Happy Birthday Darling

Happy Birthday darling
An hour older
A few years wiser
A whole day sweeter
What a special women I'm
To hold your heart
Packing up old memory
Thinking deeply how
Our love got started
Happy birthday darling
A beauty day
It seem like spring
The birds are singing
A love song
I heard this melody in my dream
Happy birthday darling
Stay forever sweet
So young and happy
With many years to come
Faith planted deeply
Hope wrapped and bounded
We'll see
What the future brings
The joy of a man and woman
In each other arms
Spreading gold as we paint the town
Happy birthday darling

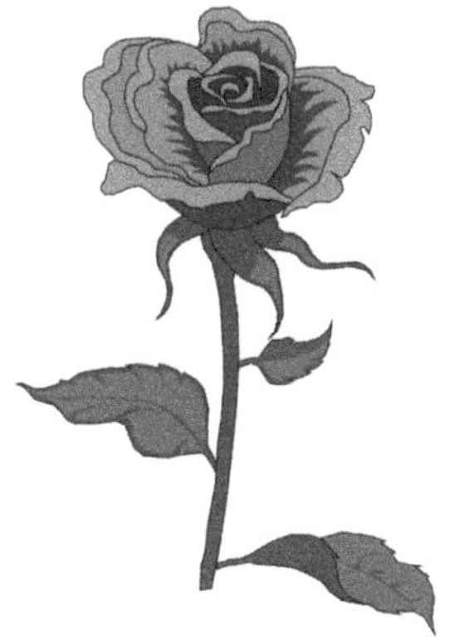

This gorgeous day of autumn. Mom as I sit in my room recalling all your jokes all the times you gave me a check you self-card. I know you are gone from this earth plain in the physical form but in the spiritual form I know you are always with me.

Thank you mom for tolerating all the good and not so good things I have done and how you endure all the not so pleasant cuts that life dealt you. Mom what a wonderful job you have accomplished. You are more than a super woman more precious than any diamond on the face of Africa

Mom I simply love you and your loving memory will never leave me. Thank you for being the woman that you were, for you have made me all that I am.

## Happy Mother Day Mom

Happy mother day mom
I remember how you held me in your arms
Happy mother day mom
Thank you for all that you have done
Holding our hands and never letting go
Prudence and virtues is what I know
Fighting all of our large small battles
Picking me up when my heart got shatter
Happy mother day mom
Thank you for keeping me from so much harm
Well mom now that you're not around
Sometime my soul crumbles to the ground
I just remember the words you have said
Trying to keep a pure heart
Sometime I forget to say my prayers before bed
Mom this one is for you
Only God know what you have been through
I love you mom
You will always be in my heart
Forever in the almighty arm
Happy mother day mom
I love you

# He said; she said

He said
She said
They said bad things about me
Show me the video tape
Show me the security camera
Well
I am here and you're there
What is the difference
Now you can hear it
Straight from the horse mouth
I am not the one who have ten, twenty, or thirty people
In or out of my house
I am not going to die, and then find peace
I want it NOW
I am entitle to it
I don't get in engage all this drama and he said, she said
Hell, I aint get paid for this drama
Nor do I have a spot on stage
Virgo by birth rights
Hermit by birth rights
Very introverted
The queen of swords by choice
I'll cut it like it hot
He said
She said
Stop lying on me
You're not invited to my house
It's plain and simple; I don't want to be bother
Please call me before you come
I will not answer the phone or door
Good luck getting in
I can't change anybody, other than myself
I stop trying long, long time ago
Peace and quiet is my motto

Stay outside with the bs and drama
Kindergarten is over with
I am not going to babysit
No grown ass man or woman
With craziness, and ton of drama
If any kind of drama went down in my house
You can bet all the peanuts in Skippy
My eyes was closed
My back was turned
People coming in and out of my house
I paid the cause to be the boss
Everybody else got to go fast.

# Hoo-Doo Luv

Stop using hoodoo
To buy love
You can't make them love you
Love is free
Love is natural
Love is endless
Love is never a hot mess
Love is sweet
Like a honey dew
Bright like the sunshine
Love make you run home
Love never will leave you all along
Love is powerful
Love is a double pane glass
Love is a fortune wheel
Love is a watch tower
Love is a time clock
It ticks by the hour
No need to use those love spells
That hoo-doo
To trick him
To trick her
Don't roll dirty
Why be
A ghetto toxic little birdy
Have some class
That hoo-doo love
Never, ever last
A go up
A blow up

The joke is on you
The love of your life is through
Love come free
Love is
Sweet
Love is naturally

# How Do I Know

How do I know
I am just a child
Learning what's being taught to me in this imperfect world
Imbalance world of
Imbalance neighborhoods
Imbalance life

How do I know
I don't know it's racist
I don't know about white supremacy
I don't know about hate for Black Lives
I don't know about hate for gays
I don't know about hate for lesbians
I don't know about hate for other races
I don't know about hate because of gender
I don't

# Humble Bumble Bee

Look at the bumble bee
They're so humble
Flying around
All day long
Smelling the flowers
Drawing the nectar
I wonder how sweet
Do each flower smell
The queen sitting on the throne
The workers busy as can be
I think I know
The life of
The humble bumble bee

# Just to Say We Care

I care
We care
Mr. Fireman
Mr. Farmer
Mr. Policeman
Mrs. Teacher
Everyday regular people
You're the people who make
Someone else world brighter
Mr. Telephone man
To the people who
Repair the broken street light
That make everything right
The restaurant cook
The candle stick maker
The counselor
The cake baker
I care
We care
Thank you

# Karma

Karma is dying
And reincarnate back
On to the earth plain
To live
Smell
See
Touch
Feel
Whatever pains you cost another man kind
To suffer
To endure
Karma can be
Good
Karma can be
Bad
Karma is
A balance of
Your deeds
Karma is real
The Pastor said so
The bible said so
You reap
Just what you sow
This is Karma
Serving a slice
Of humble pie

# Mind Trip

I went on a trip
Yesterday
I stop by body house
Body and I
Had a very long conversation
Body told me to pull up a chair
Body told me to look in the mirror
Body told me to think about
All your mistakes you made
From birth on down to prebirth
Body had a pitcher
Of pure holy water
Water that came from the rivers of Jordan
Purified and chemical free
Body offer me a cup of holy water
Body then told me to drink one cup
Take the second cup of holy water
To wash myself with it
After cleansing
Body told us by the time
We reach spirit house
All of your sins will be
Shall be wipe; and set cleaned
We relaxed for a while
We thought about all of the good times
That we used to have
As we shared pictures and looked
Backed down memory lane
Then we drove to mind house
We had a deep look at all things
Mind and I set down
To review each other
We came up with an idea
On how to work on

Each areas of life
For the highest and greatest good
Mind was feed the best of food for the journey
You can then find soul
There soul was lingering near by
Soul was then washed and cleansed in the essences of time
Soul spoke
Soul stated we need to be prepared
For spirit
As I (we) proceeded to meet spirit
Spirit is a mighty source
For spirit housed and keep
The chambers of the heart
Once spirit is cleaned and feeded
Then you have a pure good soul
Once soul is wholesome
The mind can function in excellent condition
Once the body is treated like royalty
A brand new life can began

# Mr. N.

Where are you
Mr. N
How're you
Mr. N you cross my mind
One, twice or even seven times
Thank you for your gratitude of kindness
Of course, I'm talking about B
Laugh out loud
Not B it not my fault you're so fine
Mr. N the king of inspection
You didn't have to show me any kindness
But you did
I had to travel by bus and take two trains
North Quincy to get that dough
Mr. N I hope that
Mercy, kindness, and blessings smile
Back up on you for all the goodness
That you have done
Thank you, thank you so much
The world at the moment became brighter
Good people are still around
That built your life up
When the world seem to be falling down
Thank you Mr. N.

# Narrow mind

So narrow minded
Nothing can get into it
Nothing can get out of it
Buried deeper than a sand pit
Ignorant and blind by some means
Destroying your wishes
Demolishing your dreams
By a lack of understanding
So narrow minded
You can't build the bridge
To your future
There's no work inside your mind
No hope no kind of planning
Narrow mind for life
Just love teaching other people
Your nasty way of thinking
Burdening them down by your strife
Narrow minded
Dwindling away with time
Blocked trapped
Refusing to leave the past behind
Narrow young and old mind
Learning nothing in life
You close your brain line.
Narrow small mind

# One day you'll look back

One day you'll look back
Filled with regrets
Filled with broken dreams
Filled with the what if's
Running faster than a speeding train
I tried to derail your train
Put a dynamite on your tracks
You ran wild
Chasing Alcohol
Chasing drugs
Trying to rekindle
All that you thought you missed
Traveling faster than the speed of light
Aging years beyond your time
Slow down Rose
You'll someday look back
Missing priceless moments
So priceless
The weight in gold
Can't pay
One day you'll look back
You seem unstoppable
Rose the joke is on you
Time has a destination for everybody
So do pain
Aches carry weight
Your youthfulness spreaded by wrinkles
Your game blowing like a grain of sand
One day you'll look back
How I tried so hard
Too stop you
So hard to help you

I suffer for your sake
The harder I tried
The deeper I would sank
My life flooded with pain
My mind wander
Almost to the point
Of a straight jacket
Changing lanes
All most going
Totally
Insane

# One Strange Bird

You may not ever get to know me
I'm one strange bird
I believe in human right
I believe in death to the last fight
This fair smile
Deep behind this fair face
This soprano, alto, tenor voice
In the mist of the morning
The sound changes as the day rolling on
To get to know me
It's like hunting for a lost treasure
Far away upon the wide sea
One strange bird
My mind is cool calm and steaming
My head thinking focusing and collecting
I can send so much love
Rotate time turn my hand
Turn love into totally absence
Who's that we trust so much?
No one really, no one
So the grave is a secret vault
Life is an open book
Telling only that is sometimes necessary
Burning bury and sealing the rest
One strange bird
Flocking, flying, and perching
A brief silent moment for rest
I adore peace harmony and liberty
Dislike no justice, hatred and ignorance
Cherish family close and far
One strange bird
Never making causing a up roar
An elevated mind that'll always soar
So many friends but now so few

One strange bird
Your food clothes and man is safe
One strange bird
Strolling along in life huge maze.

# No Water On a drowning Man

He's drowning
No more water please
A life saver
It what you need
Don't drown him
If you dig one
Watery grave
Just dig two
The next one will be for you
We'll sink right down
Faster that the speed of light
Dropping of the radar
Sinking out of site
Rolling to the bottom
Two watery graves
That's so right
If you can't help him
Stay out of his sight
No more water on
A drowning man
A life savcr
Indeed is what
His hand need

# One Strike

I'm so glad
That you're out of my life
No more lies
No more pain
No more kiddie games
Everybody thinks that
A break up is bad
If the person was
A trip without a suitcase
That is just one less
Stitch in your ass
A big huge one
A sore that is never done
A loose caboose on the run
Save your tricks
You silly rabbit
So long with your nasty ways
Your dirty mind
Your awful, bad habits
One strike
Sorry, you're out
I'm very impatient
I dislike nonsense
It has no room for success
It only leaves things
Very dull, dead and dense.
One Strike,
You're dead

# That Ooom Thang

It's raining
I'm feeling a ooom moment
Hold my hands
I want to run wild
Dance
In the pouring rain
It is so refreshing
It makes me
Want to do that ooom thang
You know
Ooom
You know
You should be in my bed
You should let me
Inside your blossoming head
A oom moment
So sweet in the rain
I'll keep
The rain wont tell
Nobody about
The ooom thang
Just wanting
A very special somebody
To have a ooom moment
I got somebody in mind
I can't say that yet
My ooom moment
Will get better
Sweeter
Wilder
In due time

# Other Peep Opinions

Blah
Blah
Blah
Why
You got to worry about other people opinions
Why do you have to give
A good gotdam
A hot fuck
An a cold shit
Did they wake you up this morning
Did they pay your bills
Did they feed you
The End.

# Rose

O Rose, just because you're a hard leg that doesn't mean, I can't call you a rose.

Please forgive me if I have caused you hurt and any kind of pain, beyond what my eyes can see.

We humans spend so much energy trying to please our next-door

neighbors, bosses, friends and other people.

What about the person right under our nose? Yes, our nose your spouse.

I can take some time to laugh with you.

I'll make time to smile and be more gently.

I'll try harder to be cheerful when we're together.

Rose don't get me wrong, rose, you're not the problem.

If us as human being would look in the mirror and admit that we have problems, a lot of broken homes would not be.

There is and deeper issue that lie within the surface of my skin. I wrestle with it. I battle depression, because of all the negative and nasty things I have gone through with my immediate family members.

I'm fighting negative thoughts, when I was positive and nothing or nobody could touch me. Walking on cloud 9, so high out of pure positive energy. I also used to be the eyes of the party, smack center of the attraction. Many things have changed now.

I will get back on top of everything, if it was all good then.

I was there like a moth compelled to the flame of a warm light.

Rose it's not you but me my soul has to be reconnected to the spirit the spirit aligned with the body to become one. When everything reconnects then we're happy, our lives are more open and full of joy.

I remember being a very flamboyant dresser; everything had to match, including the panties and bras. My spirit is starting to reconnect.

I want that beautiful head of hair that is long and very thick, when I walked down the street, I get compliments like is that all your hair. Of course, it's.

Rose, my hair is falling out it is dry and brittle, because the ingredients that I use to put in my hair is not there anymore. It requires patience, love, moisturizer and a lot of grooming. My skin used to be silky and smooth with that rich brown caramel color reflecting a chuck of caramel kisses.

Due to stress from these young people who want to be grown in our house.

I will be so happy when the driver of destiny pick them up to fulfill their wishes in life.

My body is no longer muscular, and ladies would tell me what a nice body I had. I sometime got offended.

Why should another lady be telling me that and making comments about my lips too?

Please Rose help me find the missing pieces to the puzzle, there got to be away out of here. I haven't enjoyed all the fun things I used to do such as open-mic, free concerts, ride the jump on jump of bus, long and continuous walks around Cookout Park.

Rose I don't need to keep a journal of my errors. You're bottling them up when you don't release the past and walk to the future. I know what I did was wrong, how many errors are us human beings allowed to make?

The mind consists of two levels a higher one and a lower one.

We have to decide which level we will park on?

Does anybody Rose always keeps their mind on the things that they want and off that in which they don't want?

Rose it's hard, task can be accomplished. A working positive mind is never dull. I have for sometimes felt like the eight of swords trapped with no way around, over or out.

There is a world outside of this shell.

In order to get out my mind has to reprogram itself, break free of negative thoughts, free from procrastination and break that mental chain that bonds me, in the blame game.

I want my old self back, the good old me not the negative one. It's wrong Rose to always concentrate on me morning, noon, and night.

Positive goal achiever must keep away from bad people, places and things.

The negative habits have to be dropped faster than a wingless plane. So far Rose we have achieved seventy percent of this task. I can expand room for improvement. A negative has two angles or side, no width or height.

A mess is just a smelly mess.

The mind can recover and find all the missing serotonin it need.

Rose, I have restored a lot of my old friends, and I'll put them back into my memory of calling list.

My entire strength is stronger than I may realize. It's not my place in life to map out anyone else future, but according to the stars to decide what it's in life you wish to become.

Rose, we all have that little girl, boy childhood about us. Even though we are adults we fear things, we're uncertain about tomorrow and what will happen. We need a shoulder to cry, talk, and lean on at all times.

Rose, sorry you had to see me at such a weak and sloppy time in our life. I was lounging around on the pity stool, trying to pick me up.

Well Rose a new year a fresh start. It's God who has provided us with the air we breathe, the food which came from the earth, the ability of using our body limbs, and created every ounce of skills that run through our mind.

Whoever said, "We can't live life to the fullest, who ever said, "we don't deserve the best life has to offer. That while it's called second chance.

Rose, we'll begin all over and accomplish all of our goals and dreams. I see the unseen, I have tasted success in my sleep, I have driven to the deep depth, and found the most priceless treasures, and I want to share them all with you Rose.

# September a cool time

A crispy fall air
A damp wet morning due
No more stinging insects
Leaving your body
Black and dark blue
All summer long
You have been on my mind
Wishing and waiting
I hope you're doing fine
It's the end off
The long hot summer days
The children are going
Back to school
A lot of homework
All work and hopefully no play
Everything seem nice and cool
New face new teachers
Listen learn follow the rules
The leaves are fallen down
Yellow red orange and brown
September a cool time
A long truck ride
To pick some plump red apples
A breezy filled sky
The warm fire logs
Burn with a zap of maple
September a cool time
The end of hot summer days
A crispy cool breeze
In my arms draw you near
September a cool time
You are always on my mind

# Sleep

Sleep
Sleepier than sleep
Flow away into
A world of dreams
Float away where
Everything is real
At least that what it seem
Sleep where you
Meet the dead
Sleep where the living
Are free and friends are near
Sleep crazy dreams
Wild frenetic screams
Night mares and horror stories
Sleep a journey
In space where only you
The sleeper can program
All of the scripts
Sleep
Sleep
So peaceful and out
The spirit leaves the body
Sometimes never to return
A rest place for my traveling feet
A break at last is what I have earn
Sleep and rest
Sleep
Sleep
Snug tight like a robin in a nest
Sleep
Sweet peaceful dreams
Everything in our world

So real yes it do seem
Sleep dreamer go deep
Sleepy so Sleep
Paint a better tomorrow
In our mind
There our dreams
Store away on
A subconscious plain
There it will forever keep

# Soldier Man

I remember this soldier man
As a young girl
Young and green as grass
Thick full sandy hair
Youthful in heart
Nothing to worry about
In this world not a single care
He stood on mamma L porch
The steps made of marble
The most beautiful material
A child could see
In a child mine
Who is that!
What in the world do he do?
The soldier man ask
What is your name?
I replied with a smile and hand shake
The soldier man had the most beautiful
Dark skin
With medal all over his jacket
My little mind was totally lost
I wanted to be like soldier man
I want to walk in soldier man shoes
I want to follow soldier man
I lost soldier man for thirty nine years
I found soldier man
We had the best times
In my life
We caught up on old time sake
So happy I found soldier man
My hero
My role model
Our soldier man
My friend for life

# Something outside my window

It rattles
It clicks
It sticks
The leaves are whispering from left to right
I think it's something goes bump in the night
Something outside my window
Is it invisible
Is it hairy
Is it scary
Is it from another planet
With scales and three eyes
A wart on it nose
A double set of teeth
A ten-inch tail
That hoots, howl, and growl
An very old cemetery down the road
The voices are not still
There is something outside my window
The blanket, the sheet, and pillow
Secure me tight
A broken wind that fly by
Outside my window
A few things that go thump and bump at night
There's something outside my window.

# Spirituality

What is spirituality
To me it is communing with the Creator
Learning to be very forgiving of others
Learning to live as one body mind spirit and soul
Church is a building and there are many titles of religion
You can go to church ten times a week and hate people of all color and creed
Recheck your religion and seek a higher God
You except to be successful but holding a grudge tighter than
A pair of butter tight glued on jeans
Your mind is a powerful thing
As you think it so shall it be
Use your mind or it will use you
Keep your mind on the things that you want
Keep your mind off the things that you don't want
I have a secret of my own
It consist of positive thinking and choosing positive people
A lot of people think of you as snobbish stuck-up
There is a saying you're know for the company you keep
If it good cut me in or cut it out
Paint your own future
Never let nobody label you
That has no place in this universe
God hold the stroll to your past present and future
After you sign a contract with God doing your journey
To this college called the earth plain
Spirituality is having a heart lighter than a feather
Repent and ask God for forgiveness and forgive other
If thou God forgive us of our little big dirty things we have done

# Strings from the Past

Do not tie me down
With the strings
From the past
For I do not
Want to sit
In the seat
Of anger
I do not want
Too drink from
The cup of bitterness
I will not ride
The waves of hate
I have come much
Much too far
Too look back now
My eyes are locked
On the present
For the past is
What it is said to be
The past
Do not tie me
Nor bind me
With old rivals
I care not to know
About them
Nor what hand in life
Has the wheel turn for them
Tie me not with
The strings from the past

My soul is humble
My mind is free
And my spirit is clean
I cannot change it
I'm living for today
And thinking about what
Tomorrow may bring
Tie me not with
The strings from the past
It is gone
Roll away with time
I wish not to pull it back
Please not tie me with
The strings from the past

# Stumble Stone

I stumble upon a stone
A short cut
Not far from home
At Franklin park
I heard an echo cry
To me a voice whispered
Come here and see
I follow my intuition
It surely guided me
The closer I got
I was in tuned and words
Dance around freely
The stone spoke
I started to feel
Light but poeteditly
It was the stone of Ralph Waldo Ellis
Speaking to me physically
Ralph words as I read them
Showered me like a blanket
I didn't see him
I felt his presence
The words that flowed
From his poem
Embraced me and
I pause to go deep
Inside my mind
I had a connection
Perhaps a flash taken
Me back into another time

Ralph Waldo Ellis
A poet voice
A connoisseur choice
I rub the stone
In my mind I mumble
Ralph we could have written
Many poems passage and themes
A great writer
A path to enlightenment
A touch of reality
My stumble stone
Didn't happen in my dreams

# Stars So Bright

Glazing at the stars tonight
Stars so bright
They light up the sky with light
Star bright
Stars shine with all your might
High above the world
Gleaming like a priceless pearl
Stars dancing in the night
In the beauty of the moonlight
I can talk to you
I feel so lucky
The big new moon
Boldly laugh at me
Enjoy the light of the stars
Darkness of the full moon
It will start to change soon
Stars so bright
Keep the sky lit by night

# Sunday's Skunk

Everybody that goes to church on Sunday doesn't have God in their heart or anywhere else. These are the one always talking about God word, and always talking about people behind their back. These are the people who wear those big huge hats and teach other people about bible and lie like a dog.

That is a Sunday skunk for you. They are so miserable and unhappy they can't stand to see you happy. They have lived their hold life in a rumble.

A Sunday skunk is a man or a woman just flat out doesn't have a life. If you had a life you would not be running to other people house and trying to control everybody else affairs.

If you don't pay people rent and your name isn't own the lease, stay at your own house for goodness sake.

Get a life, go find a man or a wife and make their life miserable just like yours. You stink so bad and no matter where you go people notice your personality and attitude and your controlling way.

Slavery still exists, but not where I live at. Stay away from me before I lose my religion. You say that you're a religious person but I can't see it. You talk about everybody of course behind their back. What you need to do is mind your own business and go and get a piece of the action for you self. That way your mouth is closed.

The Sunday skunk's always whooping and shouting amen, every two seconds.

The left door is waiting for you.

It will be no surprise to you

When you face your judgment who are you going to lie on then?

Two time double crossing fake people

Sunday skunk never have anything good to say about anybody, there mouth is constantly running. Even when they are sleep, they are still talking about people. You have to manifest this negative in your mind in order to execute the plan.

Sunday skunk is just rotten to the chore; they smile in your face and stab you in your back.

You can't be head of household at two residents. There can only be one b***** per house hold.

Plain and it is just that simple. No way around it, no way over it, bottom line. Sunday skunk have a lot of balls, when you're standing in someone else house whining and complaining about what they are not doing. Judge not to be judge. Just like you can detect somebody else little nasty habits, perhaps somebody don't like yours.

There is a geometric figure shape like a door at the entrance up front. Find it and don't come back. Nobody have to live their life to please a Sunday skunk. I know I'm not going to. That defeats the purpose of living.
Living on this earth plain and you can't enjoy life, because misery and pain, from a close relative or friend. Sunday skunk please crawl back into you hole and stay there.

# The Crowd

The crowd is going wild

The crowd is from all walks of life

The different roads that each people travel

So unique so eccentric

The crowd

# The Blazing Hot Sun

The blazing hot sun
The day has not began
O' I am so tired
The blazing hot sun
Work
Work so hard
Help me heavenly father
I can see
My ancestors crying
Wet, soak from the bitter tears
Bloody and bruised
Blood running down through the years
Blazing hot sun
Our day has not even begun
Scars
Marks our heart pain
Time healing our wounds away
Bright big moon
Waning and Waxing
A brush to freedom
Victory so sweet
Sweeter than honey on the lips
Guide us past ancestors
Far from this dull light
Working from sun up
Working until sundown
Years come
Then the years go
No more valued treasure
Lying around to enter
The golden path to
Heavenly grounds

No more tears
No more fears
No more blazing hot sun
Our time is near
Our time is done
Feeling the spirits
Of all our past ancestors
Speaking through our mind
Can't forget the past
We want to heal from it
It's a story
Roll up in time
Only memories left
Old land marks
Reminding us of a reflection of ancestors self
Blazing hot sun
Our day is done.

# The Devil Details

The devil is working fulltime
The devil is working part time
Devils, demons, and monsters
That I had to battle
This is my personal journey
The creator or what you believe in
I (we) was created in his image
God is your beliefs
I never told myself
I was a bitch, witch, unfit, or anything else
But you did
Karma come retro
What you put out into the universe
Float back where it came from
You use your money to degrade and hurt people
You took an oath before man and God
The higher beings is watching you too
It was recorded for the record
You misused your power and your authority
Well don't blame me for your
Arrogant and big headed and treachery ways
You had the Powers
To Help
To Hurt
To do or not to do
You was the protector
But the protector turns to be the abuser
Run to you
For What
You're spitting venom and spreading false lies
Do your dirt
The truth be told
I felt your blows, I felt the blows
Sweetheart you're going to be the one hurt

God got me covered in his shelter
How sweet it is
How wonderful; it can't get any better
Don't blame me for your mistake
You made them not me
Start growing up
For your own sake

# The Spirit of Boston

There's a spirit moving in Boston
I'm not talking strict about the boat
A cry for help
Soft moans in the air it floats
Drugs and murdering of innocent babies
Lime life high rollers
Sharp English and a college degree
Do I even care about me?
A spirit is moving people
Do you see?
What I see?
You got the have
You got the have not
The one's who want a lot
Bad boys
Popping each other for somebody else street
Each corner marks a death
A silent tear with a short breath
The street was there before you came
It will be there after you're gone
Why?
It has the Fore father name
The boys in Blue
Racing for you ten deep
Think my brothers
You got to change
No more jails and yellow tape
Stand up and be a man
After all who will carry the family torch?
Carrying young people of the funeral home porch
Girls on the corner
Duking it out like May West
Grabbing their crotch
What is there?

A geometric figure and a head with hair
Your brain is on ice
Smarten up don't forget to think
Not once but maybe twice
What about your actions?
You're the glue to family pictures
Do you really have any issues?
Somebody have it worse than you
For goodness sake get a life
Sometimes you cause your own strife
Count your blessing in a rows of two's
A girl should be famine sweet to the pit
You have a million dollars money making kit
There are more things in store
Than Dorchester, and Roxbury
Jamaica Plain and New Chardon courthouse
Everybody and their grandma is there
Juvenile trouble D.S.S and probation officers
Who got hope and a prayer?
Will justice ever be restored?
The spirit of Boston is moving
When will young people stop and care?

# The Spider

There is a spider
Outside
It's on the side of the porch
O' spider a hexagon shape
Spinning it webby
Making that silk
Working so hard
In and out
To catch and hold their next prey
Here is the thing
I don't see
Nothing in sight
The spider
Moving around so late at night

# The White Winter Snow

As the fire add a warm delight
The sparks from the cozy fireplace
As I watch many blankets of white snow
Fall outside my window
A whispering blanket of snow
As the red cardinals and the blue jays play
The snow will not last forever
Within days, weeks
Off the land it will go
A blanket of white winter snow

# They Called Her Ugly

Who are they
To judge anybody
When you're totally clean
Then you can talk
About me
So scornfully
This swam started to blossom
The ugly swam
Will spread her wings
This ugly swam will become
The most beautiful swam in the pond
With their noses turned up a hundred and eighty degree
Like a priceless jewel
A rare stone
Embedded beneath the
Core of the earth
A torrent of rain water
That floods the ground below
Pushing out whole diamond
Upon the surfaces
Her beauty will be flawless
She'll sparkle
As their voices become silent
Their words become swallow
With harps of shame
This picked on duckling
Feather into a golden swam
That once upon a time
They called her ugly

# Traveling Through Life

Eat
Live
Breathe
Repeat
Hoping
Just
Too live
To see another day
Traveling through life
On this rocky earth plane
Positive
Negative
How fast
Do it take
For the spirit
To exit
The body and never return
Enjoy
Forgive
Live
Let live
Be happy
Be safe
Traveling on this path called life.

# Uncle Tom

Where's the justice Uncle Tom
Sitting on that bench with your gavel
Passing judgement on people
People whom you don't know
It's easy to look inside
Through the rose color glasses
A crook is not a crook unless he steal
A swindler is not swindle unless they swindle
Laughing out loud
As time rolls around
What goes up
Surely in the heck will come down
A smile can turn into a frown
God's the one and true judge
Without a moment notice
Our whole life can unravel
Tie up
Bang up
One big ball of mess
Don't ride the high horse
Careful now
Make sure all your straps
Are bucket firm in the saddle
You're just a human being
Maybe a superior
Maybe not
Not free from guilt
Not wash completely from sin
Making people lives miserable

Dealing dirty
Passing out the four of cups
As the death card end
The judge is standing in the judgement line
The jury
The prosecutor
Standing in the judgement line
A new life
A new rule
A whole different life

# U don't Know What I've Gone through

I've stood at the four points
Of the crossroad
Smiling at some things in the past
Holding on to my identity
Trying hard not too
Make a pack with my soul
A warm caring family
A big old cold house
Mice running freely
Cock roaches racing by me
Box shipped clothes
Dollar store shoes
Borrow some who cares
Even thou they are used
I've come a long way
Learning never to compete
With no one
Happy for being me
Holding tight to my dignity
A home grown garden
All kind of fruits
Many kids to feed
Not a day of long hungry
There was always food to eat
A drill sergeant mother
Big and thick sweet and mean
Cool cold old fashion father
Using all the necessity you got
Happy as a jay bird
Even thou it's not a lot

# Un The Misfit Tree

Under the misfit tree
Standing
Sitting
Perch
Laying around
In the middle of the crossroad
Deciding which way to go
Up
Down
Side
Shall I circle back around
Don't judge me
Don't point your fingers at me
I am
We are
Just a woman
Man in a human form
Having a spiritual journey
Throw your hands in the air
Let trial and error
Bring justice
To all men
Who don't have
Blood
Sin
Spiritual crimes
On their hands
None

We all have
Trespassed against
A person
A place
Human or Animal
Under the misfit tree
Where brain
Meet the mind
To be
Or not to be under the misfit tree

# Who Money?

Money got arrested
Money went to court
Money was found guilty
Money was charged with all types of crimes.
Robbery
Rape
Prostitution
Hustling
Embezzlement
Poverty
Wealthy
Murder in the first degree
Murder in the second degree
Murder in the third degree
Assault and Battery
Homicide
Genocide
Suicide
Fraud
Racketeering
Breaking and Entry
Arson
Burglary
Drunk Driving
Kidnapping
Stalking
Tax Evasion
Gun Possession
Manslaughter
Vandalism

Sexual Abuse
Theft
Organized crimes
Hate crimes
Property crimes
Against humanity
Statutory
Inchoate
Against morality
Speeding and Moving Violations
They got money deep into jail
From the look of it
Money will not see day light
Money may not ever get out
No even on bail

# Wood Pecker

I am working over time
Busting
Grinding
Hustling
Sweating
Crying
You don't see this
You're on the outside looking in
You're looking through the rose color glasses
I have failed
I fell one time
I fell two times
Yet I rise
Yet I still stand
Yet I'll run on
Until the down right end
I have fail again
Failing mean nothing to me
It's a game of thrones
The strong is sure to survive
Writing those lyrics
Flowing the creative words
Of a new poem
Thinking
Contemplating
Demonstrating
Irrigating
Chucking away like a wood pecker
Poking and poking
Building and restoring
All that's dead let it die
Drop it right off

So hard at work
So success can grow wings to fly
Pecking away
Just like a wood pecker
Building multiple things at a time
You don't see me working
You don't see me sweating
You don't see me crying
Don't talk about what you don't know
All you'll see me is RISING.
Higher and higher soaring for the moon
Pecking away at success
Just like that wood pecker
Collecting all the stars

# Wounded Angel

I have been talked about
I have been laughed at
Thank God
It wasn't God
Who was doing the belittlement
I would be hurt
Shattered in ten billion pieces
I am a wounded angel
In the process of
A soul repair
A spirit repair
Mended from the hurt
Mended from the wear and tare
Put down, as God lift me up
He put me down
She put me down
She did low, nasty things to me
That my own birth mother Never, Ever did
I hope you have God
As you always shouting his name
Hiding behind thc bible.
I got a new flash for you
You didn't make me
You didn't create me
There for stop hating on me
Stop throwing you venomous arrows
It'll kill you
Long before it hurt me.

# You Little Nasty Boy

Steal a kiss
Seal a kiss
Keeping it a secret
Take a big risk
You little nasty boy
Behind the school
Blonde girl
Not a single clue
What getting ready
To unfold
In her little world
You little nasty boy

# Life

What have you done to help your brother or sister? Did you donate food to the homeless or did you cook a meal for a senior citizen? Did you take the time to tell that very special someone you loved them? Perhaps you should have told your neighborhood child that you would give him or her five dollars. What you give to the universe is what you get back. If you cheat, steal, and lie, then that will be your reward in life. If you do good, and regardless of what color the next human being is, give them a hand, then the universe will give you one back. The deeds of your life will be the ones to make you or break you. Remember what lessons you have learned. Did the universe teach you anything? Are you living a life of lies? The same things you did as a child, are you still doing now? Say, my brother, color does not matter; you in your thousand-dollar suit, would probably not give to a needy child to save your soul. Say, my sister or brother, the ones who hate regardless of an opinion, hate is all you know. Remember that what you give to the universe is what you get back. Say, my sister, living a fascinating life of stealing, nothing is too big for you; one day the same shoes will be put on your own feet. My brother, want a car but do not want to work for it? Did your parents ever tell you to do unto others as you would have them do unto you? This old world has gone upside-down. Blood is being splattered on the wall instead of the family name. Starvation is spreading like wildfire and say, my friend of all different colors, is it really love that got you here? Living mostly for your own needs, looking out for your best interest? My friend of all colors and creeds, what have you done to help someone in despair? Remember, this life we are living is nothing more than a huge stage, and God is playing the role in all of our lives. Never run down a person who is down today; cheer them up in their sorrow, for this world is a cold and mean world and you may be down tomorrow. Is it really hope or hate that all of our brothers and sisters cannot live in harmony? Is it really peace when the man of all nations cannot love his wife or woman? How strange is life? If I had known life would have been so difficult, I would have talked to God and told him to hide me in a shell, or anytime I wanted to leave this earth-plane let me go. In your life, what have you done to better someone else's burden?

# Southern Delight

I was born not long ago to a great set of people. My parents were not rich, but they were wonderful. My mother was a lunch monitor and my father was a farmer and construction worker.

A star was born in this little town called Plainview. The stay was very brief; we moved to another small area called Angel Bend.

Angel Bend was a small, little town that was also called Paradise. All the houses went around the block and after that was the post office, the convenience store and the dance hall. Then the woods and river were last. The school in the community was very pleasant and very convenient, and my friends were cool, too.

It was a blessing from God. I was given eight brothers and six sisters and wouldn't change anything about it at all. They were very wonderful people. Nine of them were older than I. I was the fourth oldest girl.

At a tender age, I had a passion for writing. As long as I could scribble and get a piece of paper, I was fine. Songs, poems, and plays would roll out of my mind. It's as though they were being given to me by this great spiritual being. Of course, it was God! Who else could it be? I grew up with morals and virtues, at least around Mom and Dad. I loved both of them. I got to spend nineteen wonderful years with my mother and twenty-five great years with my father.

I remember very well the echoes of my deceased parents, hearing their voices in my head as though it was a high-quality audio cassette. This impression has guided me and is forever in my mind.

I cherish my memories of childhood laughter and childhood tears, hearing and seeing the ghosts of yesterday playing over and over again in my young eyes.

Thank you Mom and Dad, for your precious, easy, hard, not-so-good ways. No matter what you take from me, you can never take away that southern dignity. I'm so proud to be from the heart of Plainville; a real and true mockingbird with a very colorful bunch of charming feathers covering my tail and will never ever push it under no tedious tree.

Pride is a very high word that this southern belle rings loud and clear with. No matter where I go in life and what star of hope I aspire to reach, I will always be me. Most of all, I am very grateful to be a southern belle.

It's not how fast you get to where you're going, but it's about never ever forgetting the stepping blocks from which you came and the people who had to stumble and struggle through both rain and fire to battle the mountain for you in order to get you to where you are today.

Yes, indeed, I will always love those special family and friends in my life. I don't have time to cause wars with them, for life is like a jigsaw puzzle and sometimes you can never find all the missing pieces. I will always be that little country hummingbird that sings again and again, holding deep childhood memories and sweet values of charity in my soul and spirit. Life is one long big highway, with many turns and curves.

# So Juicy

Dear Bam,

Thank you for a beautiful and exciting Wednesday night. As we embraced each other, I saw just as the sun that rose in the morning sky that you were tired and very sleepy. Your deep, baritone voice spoke soft, sweet words. Your full lips were sweeter than honey. They are just as juicy as a plump spring berry that has been filled with May water. Your sensational body odor; nothing of a dirty smell, but that of a soft musk. Those big brown eyes seem like a glowing Koala bear in a dark night. Your warm and gentle arms open wider than a fishing net spread out into the cold Atlantic Ocean, waiting to swallow me with all of your warmth. Oh my goodness, those sweet and juicy lips meet mine. Oh baby, you're driving me wild. My radiation level is rising higher and higher. Where is the ice?

I'm hotter than a wild cat on a hot tin roof. You grab me and pull me closer and closer. Kissing me gently and softer. Aw, baby. One kiss, then two kisses. On the third kiss, I'm yours. My, oh my, honey, put the pedal all the way down on the metal. I'm holding on as you lower your thick, muscular body toward me closer and closer to my nice and smooth-figured frame. "Baby, are you ready?" you whisper softly. "Yes", I reply.

I'm ready to be swept off my feet and whirled into a passion of forever love. Gently rubbing your hands over the pit of my May apples. Spreading the sea of love. It is as though you're spreading cream cheese on a tasty bagel. For the first time, you gently warmed your hands around your sweet and so fulfilling stick of joy and dove into the field of honey dew. Each time giving pleasure on top of pleasure. Leaving bowls and bowls of loving. So nice.

A soft and faint moan. I whispered, "Honey, oh honey," as our lips touch and kissed. As though we are two people who journeyed over millions of miles to see each other for the very first time. I discovered all the hidden secrets that held the pot of gold that I call love over and over again.

It is so marvelous; not even gold ink can write the feeling I feel. My heart is lighter than a feather. My mind is in the stage of Passion Island. I'm walking on cloud nine. Honey, promise me, please. Tell me you will always make sweet passionate love to me. Our love will last forever. I want to always be yours. If only you knew how my heart felt. I would give you valuable diamonds by the pound. Wrap my love up for you and save it in a glass jar.

It feels so good as I taste your sweet and ripe berry juice over and over again. Better than Campbell's Soup, which is "mmm, mmm, good."

Honey, hold my heart forever and leave me never. We can withstand any obstacle and walk over all kinds of hurdles. I will always remember you being so juicy. Juicy. So ripe in mind, body, and spirit. I love you always and am forever yours.

# The Store

It was a pleasant and sweet autumn day in which the world around me was running like the tracks of a speeding train. Everything was crossing but nothing coming together. So please walk with me, step into my world, and hold on.

"Go to the store and please hurry up and get your butt back in this house. You know you are not living in the country, so please be very careful and always look while crossing the road."

"Okay, I will," and he made a mad dash for the door.

I waited patiently for more than three minutes. By then ten minutes, finally thirty hair-pulling minutes tick away before my very eyes. Puzzled and worried, I called my sweet and dear cousin Erika, a very tall, young, and somewhat chunky girl who has a desire for wild and crazy hairstyles. Erika only lives perhaps five minutes away from me, just walking distance. I called Erika

"How are you doing?

"Fine," she replied".

"What's wrong?"

"I sent my son to the store and he has not gotten back yet. Erika, can you keep the girls until I go and see what happened?"

"Yes, bring them over please and go."

In my mind, the child was hit by some speeding or drunk driver and he could be laying in horrible pain and no one will tell me a thing. Then these young uncivilized thugs probably beat the daylights out of the boy and he is unable to speak or get help. Maybe he decided to go to a so-called friend's house without asking me my permission? Or at some pissy little girl's house.

'Oh my God, where is this boy?' The journey to the store was filled with anxious and puzzling questions. Questions that a mystery novelist would love to dig deep within and find out who did it and why.

It took me a brief three minutes and a couple of long, hard breaths to reach my destination. I reached the front part of the step of a store called Rite Aid.

"Can I speak with the manager?"

A very tall white man replied, "I'm the manager."

I asked, "Have you seen a little boy?

He said, ''Yes I have. Is this your son?"

"Yes it is and what seems to be the problem?"

"The security guard caught him trying to steal a magic marker."

"A magic marker?" You could have walked down the street and found one of those for free.

"Is that true?" I asked him.

"No, I was just looking at it."

"Just looking at it?"

"The security guard stated that he was looking like he was going to steal it."

"Well, it's a big difference between stealing and looking at it."

"Are you this child's mother?" he asked.

"Yes I am. Show me some proof that he was stealing and them I will believe it. Where is the videotape?"

The manager replied, "You don't need proof. Just call the police."

I thought, what a dirty rotten dog.

The security guard stared at me, I wanted to give him a good blessing out. Tell this brother his alphabet backwards. The good side of me said, 'be nice to him'. So we started to talk and I asked him a couple of questions, hoping that he would be nice to me and let my son go

The security guard asked, "What is your phone number and your address?"

I replied, "The address is wrong, but the phone is very wrong and the wrong birthday. I don't know why you are trying to get over on someone. Those plots and tricks are for clowns and right now you are making a good one out of yourself. That is the reason why you are up here rather that at home because of your clowning around."

Well fate must have planned this because I sure didn't. I stepped back and gave this brother a little lady inspection and I tell you this brother was nice looking, brown-skinned, pointy nosed and skinny, but he was a very handsome man. His teeth were white as pearls. We talked and talked and he realized that I was a wonderful person and tried to live good and do the right thing, but was catching hell trying to climb up that hill.

This brother talked with very high pride and dignity and was a real warrior and leader in his own time and soul. We exchanged addresses and phone numbers and I thought to myself, *'This lying lizard, I bet he will not call anybody.'*

The telephone rang, and guess who was on the end? Mr. Security! We phoned each other a lot and finally decide to arrange a time and date he would see me. That's right, my dream lover and friend for life. The charming, warm, loving Mr. Security. I put on my coat just to keep the clear crispy fall wind from blowing too hard against my brown cinnamon skin and put on a black velvet hat that had a pretty, but fake rose on the top.

I proceeded to walk to the destination that carried many people from place to place. The old, popular, and famous Jackson T and train station, that was everybody's good friend. I entered the train station with this seventeen-point-seven million dollar grin, grinning from ear to ear. He smiled back, his teeth were whiter than snow and his shiny, pointed nose. I looked over at him and a wild and sweet thought crossed my mind, and an impression of a sugar plum vision danced around in my head.

I wonder if he wanted an over-the-water lover or a beautiful gullible Americanized fool? I turned the door handle to the downstairs apartment and slipped in the hallway as though I was a thief coming for a pot of gold in the broad daylight.

"How are you doing?"

"I'm fine. What about yourself?"

"I'm fine, too."

We walked back to my house. I didn't know him so I could not hold his hand. Yet, we walked very close together and shared this tremendous laughter. We took the elevator up to the fifth floor. The smell of urine floated through the air as though air never existed on that side of town and water stopped running one light-year ago.

I opened the door to the entrance of my house and welcomed him in, a total stranger but a stranger who seemed to be very warm and loving. We met on many occasions, some of them were very unpleasant and some of them were very sweet, filled with honey and crying of a bitter cherry on a hot and unpredictable summer day.

There was a time when the total stranger brought me flowers and did things for me that no other so-called man did for me. He was there for me through thick and thin. He held my hands through a life and death situation. He stood around when most men would have walked away and said, 'forget her'.

What kind of man would be with a woman when she is being harassed and deprived of her most precious capsule of life? Sleep and a pot of gold leading to a stable and fulfilling joy, which I call insanity. I stated before that this brother had impeccable courage and patience.

I couldn't put up with this one no-thinking American I knew who would only pass by school because he was afraid to stop by there. Yes, you heard me right. Put a first-grade math book in front of him and the sucker would run. Better yet, you let him read 'Dick and Jane' and you will roll over with laughter. What a real clown.

This dream lover and I went everywhere together, and we bought each other gifts and held each other in our arms. I cooked the easiest and not so easy dishes for him. I thought my kitchen would hold within its walls, the dishes I created for him. We spent countless nights and days together. We were like two peas in a pod. He came to my house every single day. He would be at my house before the sun rose. He would pick me up to drop me off at college. If heaven is this good I don't want to come back. He taught me precious secrets, holding nothing back. I learned a different language I never had spoken before.

Moo Goo, my Moo Goo please help me.

I ate food of a different culture. Food of our lost, but not forgotten culture of Africa. Food like summates. It is a soft and sweet pastry that you can stuff with onions, or turkey, or beef, if that is your choice.

I have no regrets about this life and romance drama that is hanging with thoughts in the readers' mind. I thank God for letting me encounter such a blessing of a rare and thankful person as my friend. The memory will remain deep within my soul from many lives to come. God, if I can't be his mate in this lifetime, maybe the next time around you will join us together and make us one.

At this store is where I met my long distance lover and friend for life. From that day forward, two worlds came together and gripped hands as a diverse change. The security guard that could have charged this young adolescence with theft did not do it. A little kindness sometimes will not cost anybody a red penny. Forever you will be my Mr. Security.

I hope you have enjoyed my short story on my journey to the store.

# Fatherless Mammy

Let me take you on a journey. One that is far too close and could be happening in your own life. Maybe you know someone who had to walk in my shoes. The fatherless mammy is very real. Enjoy the characters and think back and remember when you were young and innocent.

Remember when you thought mom and dad would stick around forever? When cafeteria food was smoking? The guys and girls were happy to have the keys to their parent's car. Well, times have changed. Boy have they changed. The dreams of yesterday got lost in a hail of the uneducated, disobedient, and rebellious. What happened to the good old days? Are your dreams lost or sleeping? Has your dream drifted down stream? Slowly, but not quite in the dam yet. What are dreams? Are they visions of things we want to happen or the things we see happening? What are goals? Are they puddles or hurdles that we dream of crossing? Have I jumped the hurdles and puddles that I had to cross? I stopped counting the dreams that I could see and couldn't see. I just picked up my imaginary sword in one hand and my imaginary wand in the other hand. That's right! Everything that is broken in my life I will fix. I was determined to fix it. Everything that I could not fix, I was willing to cut up and send it straight to the recycle bin.

Nothing in life is considered one hundred percent fair. Let's just take a look at it. A good car, is it totally good? Your girlfriend or your boyfriend, is anyone in life really good? You really don't know until you map a person out like a lost treasure. Now we are starting to cook.

In life, who would ever thought I would be a fatherless mammy? A fatherless mammy is a woman of any age raising children all alone. A person who planned all their adolescence and half of their adulthood visualizing that one day the man of their dreams would be found. She visualized the huge house, the new car, the wealth, and the great life. A life so good your house would be on the cover of "Better Homes and Gardens" magazine some day. One of the most rich and famous women in the world.

Yes, I still have that dream. As of now I am still a fatherless mammy. Working like a government mule raising four kids by myself with no child support. Seven days a week, twenty-four hours a day. Plowing through the rain, the snow, and the human demons just to keep on going. Going into a world of different directions.

Trying hard to be somebody and have a normal life. Why is it so mismatched sometimes, if you are bad, you attract good people and if you are good, you find bad people? The one who was cut out to be just what they were put here on the earth-plane to be? That is just nothing good. To seek and destroy a real human life. Everybody has a definite purpose in life. Never call anybody a nobody, trust me. Everybody has a purpose in life and some people have a better motive than others for living. You got the hookers and hoes, you got the liars, murderers, child molesters, and serial killers. They have a role on this plane whether we want to accept the fact or not.

I have reached a conclusion. I have decided not to be bitter, not to let anger handcuff me, not to let fear keep me company. Instead, I give it my all and remember to grin and bare it and tell it the way I see it. All days are not the same. Some are better and some are getting better. Looking back, if you add everything up, it would be more valuable than gold. It is a lesson well learned. There is a top and the top I will reach, no doubt. This is how I founded my theory of the fatherless mammy. Mamma's baby, daddy maybe. Especially when daddy is not there and is not trying to be there. Useless and not worth a nipple on a bull.

I have learned to accept life for all that it is worth. Even if a person doesn't love me for who I am. So what if a man doesn't want to cherish me for what I'm supposed to be. Who gives a @#*^! and who needs his sorry ass anyway?

Young ladies, so sweet and innocent, hold on to your childhood, seek life before seeking sex. A good time does not consist of taking your clothes off and showcasing your body. Find spirituality, meditate, and/or take yoga. Talk to someone and respect mom and pop, for they wont pass this way again. Cherish family even though they are some of the human demons that you sometimes have to fight. Sometimes mistakes can't be changed but you can grow and learn from them.

I have @#%! and stepped in it. Judge me not because I'm the one who has to smell it and see it for the rest of my life. I'm not worried because it was strength that carried me this far and it will be faith to carry me even farther. This is my typical story of a fatherless mammy.

Peace, and I hope you find what ever it is that will help you to develop your mind.

# Politically not Right

What a wonderful day. A sunny, mild July evening. Blue skies and a working environment surround me as I sit down and program the highway to my life. First, cutting the blueprint to a better paying job. I'm talking about a thousand dollars or more every week. Yes, that may not be a lot of money for you or to Tiger or Donald. I'm not one of them yet. Fly back down to the earth-plane as I narrate this story for you. A thousand dollars a week would help me pay off all of my bills and for my house, clothes, and food.

As I carve the blueprint to a better job, I'm going to grab the blueprint to public schools. What a joke, a smelly bullshit joke. Having some of these teachers in the public school system is like a black family taking Cinderella out to dinner and buying her soul food, it just doesn't fit. If you think about it, how can someone paint a portrait of a place they have never been to or seen? Many of these teachers haven't been to where some of the uneducated children are coming from as far as their aptitude. To have somebody draw your hidden abilities out and tell you what level you're on when it comes to reading and math is very important. Not all teachers are bad, though. Hats off to the teachers that make sunshine out of the dark clouds and never think twice about themselves. Then you have the ones who make everybody miserable because it is their nature. Misery loves company. Watch and you will catch someone's hand in the cookie jar. Their minds are in places and on body parts where they shouldn't be. Just a little bottle of vinegar, sour as can be. I really feel sorry for some adolescents that attend public schools.

What side of the goal are you weighing? Are you being taught at a fine quality level or are you going to school to have the teachers check your name, just to say that you came to school? Who is fooling whom? Traveling faster than the speed of light on the highway to hell. Grab hold of your school supply life jacket or whatever it takes to see the future. We are going to die, simply die in our own sorrow. Wake up. Things are still politically incorrect. One absent parent with no money, is hoping and praying and trying to shape the mold to a correct future.

Tell me who does not want to send their child to a private school. Nobody wants to be raised in a single parent home. Nobody wants to live in this old world being uncomfortable, with no money. Starting from kindergarten and on through high school, a child should have the best education that money can buy. What happened to the golden old days where a teacher pours her or his soul out at the blackboard? You need a teacher to reach the apathetic student. The student must be willing to open their minds and expand their soul. Learn all that you can learn, it is all free. Be the very best that you can be and never decide to give up.

If it is dying, recharge it. A book is a very powerful thing, yet, things in this country are so politically wrong.

Teachers and students are taking the wrong path. Yes, the wrong path. Sit down and let me explain. How can a teacher slap a word on the blackboard and call that teaching? You see, this is what the apathetic student does not understand. What good is a word if you do not understand it? A teacher simply has to break it down syllable by syllable and give examples of what it means. Do not throw it on the blackboard and expect a child to learn. Everybody learns at different levels. Some are faster, some are mid-range, and some are slow. Man did not get to the moon in one day and the late great framers did not shape this country in one day. Point is, it takes time, learning is a future tool. Sharpen it and use it. You can take knowledge with you to the grave, but material things never.

So shape up America, shape up; we are simply politically wrong, sliding down the hill of the hopeless and losing control. Teach, do not be afraid. After all, what are you being paid for? To wear your nice clothes and show off or to degrade a student because of race or what the parent cannot afford to pamper them with: money, time, and affection? Stop trying to act like it does not happen. You are preaching to the choir; I have seen this happen.

Where are virtues and morals and caning? Yes, caning, no student should disrespect an adult. That is where the parents come in. An ass-whipping never killed me. I'm turning out to be the next Einstein, I'm going to be the next Mrs. Brooks and the next Mrs. Franklin. The Bible said 'if you spare the rod, you will spoil the child'. I got a whipping only when I did something wrong. My parents weren't alcoholics, drug dealers or users, they were hard working people. Everything has a stopping point. I'm sorry for all you people who feel that caning is not good. Oh well, you come down a certain street at night and watch what happens. Your car and bag are gone. Why? If the cane was in effect, this would not have happened. The jail would only be for murderers and child molesters. Not thieves and would-be robbers. So what is so wrong about spanking your child? I have another question I would like to ask, where was Department of Social Services when the slaves was getting beat?

This country is so upside down. Things just sometimes do not go according to plan. I'm judging and reading the book from my eyes and how I see it. Mom has to be mom and daddy. Fathers are making babies and moving faster than light to another bird's nest. Teachers are having lust for students. Students have the same lust for the teachers and get them to do just about anything at all, in the name of fornication, a real show of untruth and deceptions. It is simply politically incorrect.

This is what I mean, that the teachers, parents, and students of today are living in a different world then when we grew up in. To a different style and upbringing that is politically not right. Parents should be able to spank their children and not have the government interfere. When to spank a child should be a voting decision not made by the schools but by the people as parents.

It's hard as he double hockey sticks to be a parent today. Candlelight, prayer meditation and medication is needed.

Keep what you know as virtues and morals, stray not far away from your upbringing because decisions sometimes are hard in this life.

# I'm a Bird

*What is life?*
*What is a spirit?*
*What is a higher power and authority?*

I'm going to start by digging a little deeper and revealing some of the so-called truths. I'm not going to claim that I know it all, but one thing for sure I can say I know is that there is a God, a spiritual force that sits at the table of time in which I call life. There has been a God from the beginning and will be until the very end. He may not come when you want Him and at times it seems like God has totally abandoned you. You ask yourself why does God let good people get away with nothing while the so called bad people seem to go on and on without punishment? As our spirits soar and sometimes swoop down, please relate to this poem in which I would like to share with you. So think of that quiet place where you go and the spirit seems to fly; think of that wonderful place where you meditate and try to erase all your trouble away. Let the power of God or the gods lead you down the path in which you may decide what is right. Let your spirits of righteousness be your guidance to a more incredible you.

I'm a bird
A bird who is in flight
A flight to a higher power
A bird who has soared high above the heavens
A bird who has perched upon the stars
One who has drunk the water of the old Jordan River
I have no limitations.
I'm a bird who leans on the everlasting and ever living God
His name is the Almighty
I'm a bird who flies by day and I post on the roof
Of knowledge and understanding by night
I'm the bird in which the world will see
As a bird with virtues and morals
A bird who eats the seeds of life and expands into the heart of my soul.
I'm a bird in flight
I can see far beyond the night
I'm in flight, one which is a stable and very fulfilling journey
A bird who appreciates the endurance of gain

I'm a bird who sometimes can't stand this path called pain
With every package of pain, a sacrifice was to be made
As my wings push me higher and higher
The heavenly knowledge is bestowed upon me
Courage cradled me and wisdom embraced me
I must fly on
I will fly on
I will fly on
I'm that bird which watches the rising of the sun
I'm that bird which praises the going down of the moon
I'm like a bird that is very thankful for each day
For I'm the creature of God that knows not what tomorrow will bring
I'm that bird that is thankful, who is thankful yes indeed
I'm a bird on a spiritual path
I'm a bird in flight
I will soar higher and higher
I'm a bird in flight
Perched upon the understanding given by the creator
Anchored down by the virtues of the time capsules called life
I'm a bird in flight
I'm a bird enlightened by a chosen path and destiny
I'm a bird in flight
I'm a bird of the creator
I will reach my height

# Theme for English B

I can relate to "Theme for English B"
This is me, only in a different time
Learning the value of life as I go along
Go home and write a page tonight and let the page come out of you when it comes out of you
Let it be true
"Yes, it will be just that simple."
I'm an African American born in this little town called Angelville. I didn't go to school there.
Shortly after I was born, we moved to this little town called the Ben.
It was somewhat quiet and very friendly.
I went to school in the Ben up until the sixth grade. The school was very pleasant and loving.
The teacher was very strict and wouldn't mind switching your legs.
I went to middle school in this wonderful city called Treasure Hill. Treasure Hill was a beautiful city that sat on a hill. It was sometimes fun and boring.
It was fun when you traveled to a new place and you knew no one and everything is brand new. It starts to get boring when you start to see the same old things over and over again. Like animals and people.
Then I went to college in Happy Ville.
Happy Ville was a beautiful city and man O man. Let me tell you the men were plentiful and very fine.
I only went to college for one year and decided that this is for the birds.
It's not easy, but I know what is true for me at my age.
I know where I came from.
I know where I want to go.
I'm a positive African American woman with a long way to go
With few obstacles to cross in order to get to where I'm going.
Well, I like to be in love, dance and be happy.
"I love to work and read, and learn and understand life."
What good is there in a man, if good doesn't come out of his true light? Let thy works be shown.
"Being African American doesn't make me not like what other folks like, who are different races."
I like music, anything that sounds good.
It doesn't matter who sings it.
"Sometime perhaps you don't want to be a part of me."

Yes, I often want to be a part of you, sometimes.
There are times I'm looked upon as another African American
With nowhere to go and nothing to show for it
One day, I will be where I want to be.
God will grant me the happiness for hardships that I have endured.
When that day comes, give me my space and go your way.
"As I learn from you, you learn from me."
It shouldn't matter if you're older than I am.
Black or white, we were put here to teach and to learn.
"Yes, you are freer than I.
But I'm free in the heart of the Almighty."
This is how I can relate to "Theme for English B."
I'm the writer trapped in this time and event.

# Short Long Love

Who told you that love lasts forever? Wow! They lied, lied through their teeth. What is this thing we Americans call love? I saw love over and under and across the street. Judging from the middle side of the ball, love was bittersweet, sour and then invisible.

I don't exactly have a PhD in love, but on the other hand I do. Put down very hard and dumped. My love life for the past six years has been just like a young rat's @%& very hairy and bored to the norm. There has been a lot of buzzing, but the wrong UPS man is at the door, **u**nintelligent, **p**oor and **s**tressed out.

Lies of the lips. Don't hold your hand out unless you have something to give in return. You can't get something for nothing. I support myself. Most of the time, love really can't offer you anything, except for a trip to the courthouse, and a visit from the cemetery, and the social club in that I call jail. Who wants a broke lover?

I know you have heard these sayings before, "It is cheaper to keep him or her" and "those are the breaks."

I was told, "money is not everything," but I would be a flying pig if that's not a lie. You need a man that's very well stable and able to support the family. Walk with me now, do not half-step. I like to be showered with love and affection. I don't want to go on my knees and hands to beg for them either. I love a man who gives lots of hugs and kisses and if there were a hand police, I would be in jail for a long time. I can't keep my hands to myself. Why should I?

I long to be with someone special, not a temporary lover. I want to share all the cozy, warm feelings I have inside. Hold my snuggle bear and feed him bear claws with warm bear milk. Put some soft, clean satin or silk pillow cases on the bed and sprinkle baby powder all over the bed. Hold hands out in the warm May rain. Let him comb my hair. Then I gently wash his hair and give therapy to his tender scalp. Stop it girl; wake up!

I'm turning thirty-three years old and I'm more lonely than a rat, but I have nothing full-time to call my own. The only man I have full-time, and he never leaves me, is my Hewlett Packard. When I come home, he is there waiting for me at night, too. I'm ready to have contact with a real human being, not someone from the metal world.

I like things that are blue, never borrowed. And he doesn't have to be that old. That is my dream of a man. Especially when they are very wise and ready to settle down. I like for a man to keep his mouth closed. Long after the thrill is gone, only a boy would reveal his most precious secrets and share his wildest imagination with no one other than a very devoted friend, if you can find one roaming on the face of this earth. We have a lot of them on the left and right who want to, and pretend to be real.

I like a man who knows exactly what he wants and feels very secure about himself. One who watches his weight and his health. One who is very bright and well-dressed. One who has his brain in the right place. Not one who is thinking with his manhood, if you know what I mean.

I want a man to be my friend, and lover, and partner before marriage. If everybody followed that procedure, there would be less broken hearts and corrupted minds, minds who think all women are hoes and ground dirt. When I give love, it comes from the bottom of my heart and I'm very sincere and give it my all. I will make sure that I shower my sweetie with love and affection that comes straight in his direction. I put my whole soul into it, that way, if we ever said goodbye, I would have no regrets at all.

I decided not to give my all to anyone else unless some love and affection comes speeding in my direction. I'm not the love collector. I refuse to chase anything around, except money. I have a very short fuse for nonsense and craziness. I get frustrated real quick and then I move on.

I love for a man to give me control of his everyday little options. I love to pick out his clothes and cook his food and help him with the things that he needs to be reminded of one hundred times. I like for a man to ask me what I need. I have this thing called pride that gets in my way and blocks me and ties me up in captivity. Most men have no idea or clue on how to love a woman. No clue on what she likes and doesn't want. I see why some women turn to other women for love and a long-term relationship. I like for a man to automatically give me money, but nothing in this world is for free. After all, I want support from the one person who cares so much about me. Freedom is not free, nor is religion.

Once upon a time, I had a friend who would give me anything I wanted. I let them go only to have nothing special again. Many times I wondered if I was on drugs like Prozac or Ritalin. I thought to myself, *Gosh, you need your own personal tree, one that kicks your behind every time you do something crazy and wrong.*

Things don't always have to be old for the romance to be better. My goodness, it is great, like Maxwell House coffee, its "good to the last drop". I remember once upon a time, I was with this associate who went downtown. I could not contain myself. I giggled all over the playground. I felt like an angel in heaven with a bowl of buttery popcorn. Every limb in my body trembled with pleasure and I was not willing to share them with anyone. I felt like a pirate with a million dollars worth of gold. When we were at the playground, he would blow a breath of fresh air into my flower garden and I would fall down on the ground with chills of passions.

Like I stated before, I'm tired of being in front of the computer. I want contact with a real human being; someone who has real life in them.

I was told by a close associate of mine that if I put my car in slow drive, I might get what I want. In some ways, I shouldn't pop out a list on the third night and have a marriage proposal all planned out for the poor guy. I didn't mind letting a man know right off hand what I wanted. Then I started to think. What if one approached me with a quick marriage proposal with wedding plans laid out for me? I took three deep breaths, I mean really deep. I said, "That is really scary and wild."

No, I have not ever been on Ritalin of Prozac so stop trippin', all right! Now, I'm like the age of wine and the speed of a tortoise; I take my sweet time no matter what. I wait patiently. I refuse to rush into anything with anybody. Most of the time when I tell people that I don't have a serious relationship, they want to laugh.

First of all, keep your hands to yourself. My father whipped my butt twice in his whole eighty-two years. Mom rocked that butt from coast to coast.

@#^$% beatings are off my list permanently. I like things neat and organized. I don't know whether I will ever find a man to ever put up with me. For decades, I was silent and all of a sudden, the spirit of nagging came over me. I think it is the case of wanting someone to be with. I despise a talking man who never shuts the hell up; it's scary. I tell you, honey, it's worse than a horror movie.

I know deep within my soul that love doesn't hurt. If they raise their hand to hit you, then they never loved you at all. If they let you walk away, then love blossoms from the soul of that person's heart and soul. Love is beautiful and if you have to do bewitching things to get a man, then what type of person are you? You know that mumbo-jumbo: the New Orleans style and other witching cities that cook up a spell for how to get a man anyway they can. Mom told me a million times, "Child, you can never buy love." Trust me mom, you did not lie and I wouldn't try either. Not for all the money in the Bank of Beantown.

Remember, your family and God loves you if a man or woman never loves you again. I guess over the course of time, I will know when I have found the right one. Mr. Perfect, not just the memory of someone whom I used to love with a picture added to the photograph book collecting dust.

Sometimes I think Cupid was mad at me and punished me badly. Cupid, let me give you some advice before you draw back your bow; make sure that his heart is pure and clean and his head is installed with brains, not in the freezer temporarily frozen and needing to be unthawed. A person can look so good on the outside but so impure on the inside. Truly, I can live without that type of lover. But I can daydream all night long about this perfect man who will cherish me like a queen. Call my name as though it was music from up above. A man who will do almost anything for me without any explanation needed.

I want a lover who appreciates a woman for the small and large things in life. Like me, I would thank my friend for a simple piece of brown paper bag so that I just don't nag some of the time. I nag and ask for help and think about our future and lovemaking.

I hope you have enjoyed this short and somewhat romantic, down-to-earth, so true-got-to-be-real, little story. I hope you find the man or woman of your dreams. One who will shower your life with love and affection forever and ever.

# The Lover's Hand -Part 1

What are expectations? They can be an idea of what you want in a friend or lover. Expectations can be small; they can be large. Whatever the situation may be, you decide. I have an expectation for my lover's hands.

# Lover's Hands

One day when I was gazing at the morning sun, a transparent shadow stared at me. As the sun rolled away and the wind whispered sweet words of love in my head, there appeared a handsome man. He stood about 5' 9" with a golden complexion and gray eyes. He was wearing a dark-blue uniform and a thick leather belt in which he carried a gun, and other items that a man of law enforcement would carry. Well, the badge number I can't reveal. I will leave you guessing. This man was super.

I felt this strong electrical energy around me. Please God, please don't let me pass out. On the second hand, would he give me mouth to mouth resuscitation, or would he just call 911? Do not wake me, do not wake me. Yes, I'm dreaming. He has those lazy, drop dog eyes. He looks so tasty. I can put a cherry on top of him. I want his mind, his body, and his soul. A breath of fresh air flew over me as if I were a paper doll. I could go over and say hi. Then I could build a cage and hide him with the key. Wherever he goes, I will follow. I will follow. I have to be there. No way around it, no way over it. Yes! Move over miss, don't look at him. You got it miss, don't even think about it. He's all mine. Old sweet lover, these are my expectations. Call me, honey, I'll come running. Give me your hand and I'll be yours. Give me your heart and never worry again. Give me your last name and then I'll be your wife. Joined together forever. Then we'll ride away into sunny skies and rainbow nights. This is what I expect of you, lover. I expect for you to fill all my needs, wants and desires. Happy as happy can be. Tell me that you'll love me forever. I love you too, lover boy.

# Weeping Widow

Weeping widow, old weeping widow, you have cried yourself dry. There are no more tears left for the road ahead. It was a dreary and unforgettable day in April when my best friend went away. So far away that I never got a chance to say goodbye. The only thing my poor heart got was a teary soul. Wild tears of a clown smiling on the outside, while my heart was drowning in sadness. My dear friend has gone into the arms of Almighty God, forever.

I never thought that my friend would ever leave me without saying goodbye. I'm sitting here in my room, weeping. Crying like a young weeping widow. I blame myself. He asked me to get back with him. It crossed my mind to say, "Old bitter heart and sweet soul, were you really that good that you could have taken the once upon a time love of your past back?" A slow but very sweet person is own his way home I will cherish him forever.

Oh weeping widow, I'm so young to have a friend caught up in the rapture of death. One thing about death, it doesn't discriminate, it irritates; it strike down the one of whom we love and care about. Almighty God of heaven and earth, be my guide of heart, mind, body, and soul. Chase old death far away.

Oh weeping widow, I will not yowl for you anymore. For my eyes are tired and my heart still as a lake. Old still water, turn your tide and bring back joy and laughter. Old weeping widow, I want to dwell on the good times and wash away the bad times and forgive all the flaws of yesterday that this poor soul has committed; bitter words are very few. Oh weeping widow, I was angry, so angry on that breezy April day when my good friend flew away. He put on his wings and took flight. He flew away when those close to him were not around that day. My soul wonders, why me? I prayed to Almighty God to let this friend of mine stay. If I made you cry anytime in your life, please forgive me. I thought of the time when I should have taken my sweetheart back. I thought of the time when he also broke my heart into three parts: love, closeness, and distance.

Oh weeping widow, what shall I do? I have a dear friend departing this world and journeying to another. A friend who was so gentle and kind; we did everything mutually. We were like two peas in a pod, wherever I went he was there also. I picked out his clothes. I was the one who cooked his favorite food. We called each other constantly, making sure that the other person was reminded of the love we shared for each other. I was the one who gave him money when he was running low on funds. The woman who laid beside him and listened to the beating of his heart and the rumbling sound of his sweet and acute snores. I was the one there for him when we shopped for the food of our taste buds and cooked them with the hands that rubbed his aches and pains away.

Oh weeping widow, am I so proud that I can't cry? No, I'm not. Loneliness is nobody's friend, neither is sorrow. For, the both of them need a shoulder to cry on.

Oh weeping widow, I'll always love you in memory, mind, and soul, as the widow was laid to its final resting place. I spoke softly, "May peace be upon you." My heart throbbed as my eyes sobbed.

A very close friend said, "Come over and meet the love of his life." *No, I don't want to meet her.* Rage grew deep within. It was a rage of sheer madness. How could a person be so mean and cruel to another without a good cause?

Lady, look what you did to this man. This is the man that I loved at one point and time with all of my heart. This was my very best friend and my lover. I was told that everything comes in threes. The first one got married on me. The second, honey bunches of oats, decided that life over here on this side wasn't worth living anymore. The third one, well guess what, I will spin my golden web and catch him. I will treasure him as though he is a priceless diamond. It took me a long time to get over this shocker. Man did it hurt. Love is love when you break up with a person and hold them deep within your heart.

Oh weeping widow, you turn away because of being hurt, your heart is being split into millions of pieces and no surgeon could ever perform a heart operation to repair it. I feel so guilty and down about the whole thing.

I cherish the fun memories I had with him. Rather than dwelling on the past flaws and hidden, sleepless nights. Remembering the things about him like "The Bay," "The Store," and other interesting poems and stories that will keep my heart full with laughter for the rest of my life. It is a friendship that will never, ever die. Old friend, I wrote these few words for you. These words warm my spirit and elevate my soul. As I listen to the still water of time.

# Forever Your Friend

Forever your friend
This bond that we have
No knife, stick, or brick
Could put it to an end
I learned a lot of things about you
Your laughter
Your tears
Your joy
I gave you a pillow
To always cry on
A helping hand for tomorrow
I carried you
When you couldn't walk
I chatted loving words
About you whenever I talked
Forever I'll be your friend
No words of hate or bitterness
Will rob me of my treasure
A friendship so precious
A bond so clear and deep
No ruler could measure
A living story will be told
Open like a gift box
Your name, your life
Inside my story will unfold
You will always be my pal
Nat
Your dear friend

# Garddatha

It was an exciting and wonderful experience getting my first apartment. It was the hot, robust month of August. Life was fine, until a bunch of hoodlums started to stick their nose somewhere they shouldn't go.

Garddatha had her share of ups and downs. Living in this slum called the city. Garddatha has never in her life seen so many ignorant people. Most of them are blinded by the way of mankind. They are uneducated, unorganized, and misunderstood.

Most of the women want to hang out of the window all day and gossip, looking like Aunt Jemima on the pancake box, spreading lies and fixing up goofer dust to destroy someone else's life because of jealousy and envy.

I, Garddatha, had to go back and relive my life. I would ask God to forgive me for all the wrong that I have done, and never, ever send me back to the Jamaica plain. Forgive me, Almighty God, if I have made someone angry and don't know what I have done. Garddatha knows that she has not been an angel; Garddatha has not been a devil, either.

Some of the people I made suffer, asked for it. They had no business sticking their noses somewhere they don't go; I should have rung this dog's neck, named Rob. There was this other heifer who didn't weigh a hundred pounds soaking wet, with ankle weights. It was by the grace of God and my kids that I didn't kill her, or shove her out of an open window, so she could hit the pavement like a paper-thin sheet.

This is why I hate that I ever set my foot in this slum.

I like to live and let live.

I'm a very loving and giving person.

Please don't wear your welcome out by knocking on my door and asking, "Can I borrow this, can I borrow that?" What do I look like to you, a long lost friend of the Jeffersons?

Yet, I feel very isolated. I keep away from people. Trust me. It's for my own good. Some of them are not worth a penny with a hole in it. Life is a real yo-yo and you really don't know where you are going to go. One minute you are up, the next minute you are down.

Please don't come to the slum looking for a man. Men here are the most evil, wicked, low-life, rotten bunch of @%*holes that I have ever known.

If I had a magical wand, I would change a lot of boys into men. The men in the slum want to stay with a woman, eat up her food, and live off her for free. Just like a tick, sucking up everything he can get and giving nothing in return.

Most of them are down right sorry and lazy and don't know the meaning of work, if someone gave it to them on a golden tray. Hanging on a corner, most of them are like

Johnson and Johnson, loaded with drugs, and they have never seen a high school except from just passing by it.

Garddatha knows that she is dealing with a pain in the @%* in which I'm ready to get rid of. When I was with this lazy piece of flesh, he was not satisfied. Now that we are apart, he is trying to have a golden calf. I think he should.

Now that the shoe is on the other foot, Garddatha wants to make this bastard suffer like a howling dog. A dog that has been hurt and racked with heart-throbbing pain.

Garddatha is very loving, only if you let her be.

Walk over her and you will have a fight on your hands.

The slum is no place to be.

If you were born and raised there, that is cool.

Garddatha advises no one to live in the slums.

Now Garddatha had a new look on life.

You could not pay her enough cash to go with a bean-eating @%* hole. She wants a deep talking, smooth loving, energized, over the water lover.

She was told they are very sweet and that they know how to love women and treat them right. They work very hard and you really don't have to break your neck loving a pre-paid dummy, and getting no love in return.

Call me anything you want to, but you are not me and you don't know what I had to go through, all because I didn't listen to that inner voice telling me that this cat was more trouble than good. For those of you who have ears, please hear me. Let the words of my mouth be heard and my heart cry out for that inner peace.

In the meantime, Garddatha will live for today and pray for tomorrow; God has bestowed his blessings upon her. Feel whatever is in your heart. Let it be real.

Garddatha will not let her new lover know just how she feels from here. There will not be any more tears and lonely teardrops; there will not be any more lying, cheating, and back-stabbing. There will not be any more uncaring. I found myself a lover more precious than gold, a lover sweeter than a black berry. So juicy I can taste him from across the room.

Garddatha will sit on her throne like the princess that she knew she was all along and talk to her true friends, wishing them love and happiness.

Stop, think and please listen to the inner voice. Don't make the watery mistakes that I have made.

Be happy, stay positive

# The Old Thrill

As we head into a new year, a new millennium, I was thinking long and hard about the good old days.

The days when a bag of sugar did not cost three dollars. The days in which time rolled on without waiting for anyone to call it or be still. The days in which time was the last thing anyone would worry about. Everybody loves one another or they just pretended.

The days in which platform shoes and bell-bottom pants were the norm and afros were the past, present, and the future. Hand-me-downs were the key to shopping problems. You wore just about anybody's clothing that would fit you. So what if those pants were plaid? Washing machines and clothesline are the solution.

Where did those good old days go to? The days in which candy cost one cent. Cooking was done strictly on the wood stove, and food was plucked straight out of your own garden, and the soap for washing was hand-made, without a doubt.

They had dances like the mashed potato, the alligator, the twist, the monkey, the dog. The jukebox was as funky as can be and the hits were as spicy as an old batch of collard greens.

The music was the key to the universe with the Temptations, the Supremes, the Drifters, and those other groups that had class and soul. I tell you, when those cats sang, afterwards you still heard their voices echoing inside of your mind and soul. I would love to go back in time and trade places with some who were there with the cats from Smokey and the Miracles, and the Temptations, the Chantels, and others. The coolest place in the world to hang out was Motown. I would love to trade places with somebody who walked there. I'm mad. Why did I miss everything? Then again, it's for the better perhaps. I know deep within my heart that the good times would still be rolling with all those hot, cool cats that I was fascinated with.

The days in which you could go to school and wouldn't have to worry about another fool storming into the school, shooting up the place because he didn't get an A, or the girl of his dreams was swimming around in someone else's fish bowl. Those days are gone. Excuse me, I have to write how I feel. Unlike these youngsters, who never talk about anything but somebody's mother, and who call a woman a bitch, which is short for a female dog. Then on the other hand, they are talking about who they are going to smoke (kill with a gun), over somebody else's street.

Where did the good old days go? Where sex was as wild as the flower that grew by the country road? That illegal drug you call a blunt was the key to a broke person's heart. It was very pure and fresh, getting the best of quality without those harmful chemicals in it. The good old days in which the young heart was free in mind and spirit. The crisp pure air that was in no way, shape, or form contaminated with cancer-causing dust. Wow! Take me back.

I'm going to have the biggest, old party that anyone in their whole life has ever had. I'm going to invite all of the living, legendary singers. I'll be paying a special tribute to the ones that have passed on into the spiritual world. I'm just a young fan of Motown and will remain that way until the end of time. I like a couple of things that are old, as long as they have values. I like old music and jewelry. All right now!

I know deep within, I'm free and like the thrill of the old, but golden days. They hold memories deeper than the hidden treasures of the sea. I'm the melody in which I write, so sit back and enjoy reading my hidden treasures.

# Short Long Love
# Part 2

I'm sitting here with deep thoughts of sugar plums and chocolate rum running in my head. Ideas so sweet are running across my mind. Wow!

I have the desire to be cuddled, touched, hugged, and kissed until I turn myself into a princess. Guess what? With who? I don't have anybody to call my own nothing to write home about or put their name on an old postcard. Never mind a new one. That is about to change with a dramatic passion. I sometimes drift into the past and drink the wine in which the bottle has been empty for a long time. In some words, I recall to myself, *what if what could have been, had been?*

Oh well, I feel like a billy goat in a pepper patch on a new summer day. This older cat is purring at my door step. What will he turn out to be? A tiger or a gentle pussycat? One thing for sure, I'm playing for keeps and there is no free cat food around here, Buster.

The truth is that any fish will swim in your tank and eat if you let it. Time will slowly reveal all hidden flaws. This is one smart, cunning, stunning, talking, young woman. I'm so smart at times, but I don't think sometimes.

What is wrong with putting your hook into the fish that your heart so desires? I tried to reel this other one in, my same age. It was like trying to teach a baby how to speak a different language. It was unreal. Well, that is what happens. Some women never want a man until you get him. We got along real good until the ghost of his miserable ex started showing up.

The hand of hurt was upon him and only time could wipe this pain away. We had each other. I was the summer rose in which grows wild out on the clear blue sky. He was the autumn air that takes your breath away until these other desperate females are burning for a man. The ones who really don't want to see you with anybody. This heifer was out charming him like a bum after a wine bottle. If the oven was displaying chocolate or any other flavor, he was willing to sample it. He stated clearer than a bell on a wedding day, he doesn't want to be with only one woman. *Good luck*, I said, deep within my mind. I want a full-time lover not a part-time one.

I'm Miss Cool Water and I will stay that way. I'm natural and refuse to change for anybody or anything. Oh yes.

# Naked City

I was born and raised in a state where the smell of blood still stinks when the wind blows, and the ghost of my ancestors call me from time to time, and their spirits still play in the hallway of yesterday's dreams. Life was grand and was a supreme gift given to me on a silver spoon with me knowing it. A lifestyle of cleaning and little else to do other than going to the house of knowledge and packing your brain, as if it were a sponge, absorbing all the wisdom and understanding you can put in there.

The other duty was to go to church, the house in which all the glory-glory sisters would strut their dazzle and jazzy style of clothing and hats. A house in which the spirits took control, and made them wind and fall to the wayside, and run with the Holy Ghost. Some cry and some scream and some even moan, while giving praise and thanks to God.

Coming from the heart of love, I never really encountered that other group of people who hate you without cause. It was not the white people that I had to worry about, but my own kind. The country was slamming. Slamming from the fact that it was so peaceful and quiet, man it was quiet. Once in a while, I would see a white person. They would speak and wish me well. In my younger years, some white people moved in our neighborhood and even became members of our church. In fact, one of them became the pastor. He would preach so hard, until he turned cherry red on hot summer days.

Life still remains the same in this old peaceful, still ghost town; a dull and lonely country. Oh God, when will I ever leave this place?

I graduated in June, on a hot day that was so hot you could cook eggs on the sidewalk. The school which I attended was always in order and the principal had control of the crew quite well.

Hanging around like a knot on a log and debating what to do, I decided to take one year in college in a somewhat cool town called the Ville. Well, let me tell you this little story, life here is just like being in a box of Argo starch where things are not going nor coming. I tried desperately to enlist in the ROTC and missed the test by three points and was sad for months, telling my pretty little head how I didn't know how to process it.

In June, I talked with a girlfriend. She said, "Well, you should come up here to the town of Beans."

Like a ghost who fears holy water, I skipped town. One day I was there, the next two days, my whole world was taking a completely different turn. A turn in which there were faces with no names. A world in which my mind was free, but the spirit was locked up, and the body was trying to adjust to the bitter cold world which lies just outside the door. A door in which, if you are not careful, you can open up Pandora's box and unleash legions of demons of life.

This is my version of the naked city. I hope you have enjoyed this short and heart-thrilling story.

Living is a part of happiness and virtues.

# The Big Forties

I hope when I reach my forties that I will be very pleasant. Cool and sassy indeed, stylish and rich. I will not be like some people who tell you one thing and then do another. I think men go through "mental pause", but fail to realize what is happening to them.

You know those people who I'm talking about, the ones that look at you as if a spaceship is coming to get you. I tell you, I have never in all my life seen so many grumpy and snobby people.

Some of these people in their forties act like some kind of sleep disorder has altered their brainwaves. You ask me and I will tell you it's scary to the norm. Some of these people seem to be very jumpy and, on the edge, sometimes. They snap at any little thing and they very certainly laugh and joke with you. They walk around like the universe will drop any minute. It will cost them some money to smile. My God, hear my cry. I don't want to be that way.

I know both men and women go through some rough stages in life, but hurt to some people seems to be forever. Let the bloody situation go. Move on with your life. Remember, nothing lasts forever.

Some of these people that I know are like a windstorm and are unpredictable. They will change in a heartbeat. I have something for you, some medicine that the doctor can't prescribe to you. It's called peace and meditation. That's right.

Some of them think they know every cotton-picking thing there is to know up under the sun. Do you hear me? I said up under the sun. They always give advice, but they can't listen to anyone else's opinion.

We all have a different view of life; while the teacher teaches, he or she can also learn. As I learn from you, I'm willing to open up all communication lines for you, rather than being the talk of the town and not letting your mouth fail you. Talking so much, you probably tell all your secrets in your sleep.

I wonder if your mind is at ease. Once again, it takes two people to be successful. After every good woman or man, the other will not be too far behind.

The only time they know you, is when they want a favor. Until then, who gives a cold ice cream cone about you? Please save the drama for acting school. You are not entertaining me. I'm hip to your bag of tricks, Homey. Stop throwing those bricks at me, calling me, young pissy blinking blank. I'm a writer. I can only write what I feel. So lighten up, will you? After all, it's not so bad. After all, I would like to give credit to the one and only person who created us for allowing me to be blessed with such a special gift; the gift that many bright and wonderful people were given.

Change the things that you can and brace the one you can't.

# Landlords

As I sit here, on this clear and crisp all hell's night that I call Halloween, I have lived in so many places and boy, do I have a story for you. Honey, you are going to get it. So pull up your chair and put some extra logs on the fireplace. It's going to get hot up in here.

I used to live in this neighborhood, and I tell you, it was like a deck of jokers, wilder than an African cheetah. In the "Plain," the maintenance was fine, but the landlords were very unfriendly and had an attitude that Spic and Span couldn't clean. The work order was perfect and I gave them two thumbs up for the job, which was well done. I had other problems, but no one did anything about them.

I was harassed for a whole year by a sick, uncivilized, deranged puppy. If punishment would go undone, I would be the queen of hurt. I would be the lawn mower and I would cut a whole lot of things other than grass. Move over Lorena Bobbitt, because I'm a sister with an attitude.

I used to live on the Rock and the landlord there didn't do jack nothing. Lazy boy, you're talking about lazy, that sorry son of a joke! He couldn't repair a cracked wall if someone gave him a chisel and free lessons. Well, the house had roaches running around playing hide and seek and the mice were so cool that they would steal chicken bones out of the trash and jump from the floor to the stove and hop to the refrigerator. These were not any ordinary mice. They had to be cloned and trained for this; I'm talking about rats in the hood. All they needed was a handkerchief around the forehead and a knife. The stove only had two working burners and no oven. It's a shame that some landlords live like kings and queens and let the tenants go undone. They abuse and misuse the tenants for everything they are worth and then some. It is just a matter of time. If they don't see punishment in this life, the next one will surely be for them with victory. You can rest assured, what you give to the universe is what you get back, without a doubt.

I also had an apartment with the same landlord. I tell you, somebody should have warned me. This house was very big, I'm talking gigantic, but old. My oh me, you want to describe a hole in the wall. You would faint in the summertime and freeze in the wintertime. The gas bill would be anywhere from 150 to 200 dollars a month. The landlord knew that this house was cold and very raggedy, but yet he still wanted the rent. He should have rented this icebox out to an Eskimo or someone who was not hip to his undermining and web of lies.

The other hellhole I went to was on the Hill; the house was very beautiful. It was simply gorgeous and was what a girl's dreams are made of. The only problem I had there was that the landlord just didn't care about a thing but collecting his rent, which is not fair. If someone had a problem, it should have been dealt with. Soon, I will be free from all this bathroom waste.

The neighbors are very rude and disrespectful. They don't have anything that smells like home training. I can recall I was so sick, my God, I thought that I was going to die. These ill-mannered, no home training people refused to be quiet. I did what I had to do, I called the boys in blue and things got a little better, and then they reached right back into their bag of tricks. Performing and making a three-ring circus. Each time was getting louder and noisier. The thing I couldn't understand was that their mother was there so was that sorry being they call a father. I'm not downing anyone, but laws need to be passed for people who don't teach their children manners and home training.

The landlord just doesn't give a good, hot crap, not as long as he has his money and his family is well taken care of. I told the landlord a million times that the noise was unbearable, but he did nothing about it, which is more than a crying shame. There are things that words can't describe. I'm talking things that are not suitable for television.

I'll be more than glad when I'm free from these rude, disrespectful people and this sorry-@%& landlord who thinks I complain too much. Well, my friend, if that's how you feel, then you bring your comfortable cozy-*&# right over here and tell me how <u>you</u> would like to hear kids running over and over the floor at night? Just to get back at you because you asked them to be quiet. Tell me, how would you like to have people in and out of the front door at night, opening and closing the door? How would you feel if it were you? You can easily talk the talk and pretend to walk the walk if you have not ever experienced it. I'm not used to having this entire mumbo-jumbo going on. I like peace and quiet and I want it soon. I don't have to listen to anybody else's kids running around like wild animals, both day and night. As far as the landlord goes, if the place went up in smoke, believe you me, I won't complain about it. So you should put a guard to your mouth and be more careful of what you say.

I am so sorry that I feel this way. I'm telling it exactly how I see it and I make no apologies for it. There comes a time in everybody's life when you wish you never said, did, or followed through on a matter or situation. Well, my dear readers, I'm trapped in this web of dissatisfaction and refuse to take it. I'm telling you as the story unfold, so don't blame me for any of this mess. I guess the only way to true satisfaction is in the mind of the dweller.

As for that landlord, I wish I never see him again nor meet him in either this life or the next one. I mean this from the top and bottom of my heart.

I'm not bitter or angry, but please don't knock me for feeling the way I do and I'm sorry, but I don't mean to step on anyone's blue suede shoes. I certainly don't want anyone stepping on mine. So give me my room and go in peace, live for you and I'll live for me

Love the one who loves you.

All the slum lords should be forced to live in their own houses, it would be justice.

# Computer Teacher

*Question:* I wonder why this teacher is working us so hard?

Answer*:* I believe students come to learn how to learn. After learning to use the computer, they will find more self-confidence.

*Question:* Will we ever need this hand cramping mind-boggling stuff?

Answer: Probably not. The hand cramping is going the way of the horse and buggy. But the confidence that comes from learning to control, take control of a horse and buggy, makes what follows easy as pie.

*Question:* I wonder if this teacher will ever remember a name or a face?

Answer: Yes. Teachers devote their lives to their students. I have no other career than helping students believe in themselves.

*Question:* Is Mr. Shinger giving us this work to help or is he just being mean?
answer: The work you do satisfies your need to prove yourself and it satisfies my need to feel productive too.

*Question:* What would my grade be?

Answer: An "A." You get from a class whatever you put into it. It's my job to see you give your best effort.

Mr. Singer thank you for seeing beyond our point and giving us what we needed instead of what we wanted. That's a lot of desktop publishing.

Click, click, click
Drag pull give it a tick
I'm flying through desktop
Write a poem or watch the girls shop
I can create bulletins and flyers

Send a telegram to a good homebuyer
Oh how desktop opened my world
I'm flowing like a priceless pearl
I'll give credit where credit is due.
Thanks to my computer teacher Mr. Hue
My uncertainty and fears are gone
Me and my computer are on a throne.
I'm happy I took this course.
Learning understanding that's my source
Mr. Singer your work and teaching are not in vain
Edit, spell check, print it, that's my game
Click, click, click
In my memory forever will it stick?

# How Long

Dear Bam,

Today's not so cold; it's a snowy day in March. I started out this morning dragging like a little, brown turtle. Throwing two apples into a CVS bag. Slipping on my garments for work, telling the kids how the day is supposed to start off. Sometimes, an order is obeyed very promptly by them. Gently putting my brown jacket on my shoulder. Quickly checking my watch for the time. I'm trying to make it on time. There's a fruit basket in my mind; nothing and things ever, ever go dry inside. Mission accomplished. The kids turn back to their room before their final nap.

I grab my bag and zip up my jacket, and off across the street I went. I feel like one of the Boston Marathon runners. I have to run to catch the bus. These 22 buses makes me sick. They are never on time and the service from Ruggles to Ashmont is awful. Where do they get some of these people from? Somebody needs to tie a brick around the bus driver's feet. I think he is from a different country. There are no cars around. This bus ride is like a double can of sardines.

One good thing that gets me going and awake is thinking about you. Wondering how long are we going to be together? There are times when everything seems too good to be true. My mind is like a freight train running away with me. I'm digging too deep and hard.

The phrase "how long" stuck with me. I'm so in love with you and I care a great deal about you. Sometimes when things are dark and gloomy, you bring sunshine into my life. The stars sing to me and the moon bows to me. Yet and still, this sweet but faint voice floated through the air, "How long will this last?"

I'm not losing it yet; my full, sweet lips were glued and could not utter one single word. A second flash hit me. I gently scratched my head and let the inner voice speak to me again. How long?

Still in denial. Was this voice speaking to me about my living conditions or simply before life offers me all the sweet rewards that I work so hard for? How long will I have to wait before I catch happiness? Will I have to be like a thief in the night and steal it when it is not watching? Somebody please tell me, I don't know what to say.

I feel aimless, wondering about this voice that I keep hearing over and over in my head. Flashbacks of the past haunt me.

My eyes are closed and I am lying in a very relaxed position. So relaxing I'm drifting into the land of sleep.

While I was asleep, I had a vision. In my vision I saw two glorious white doves, a pink heart and two gold rings. What does this mean?

How long will it take? One year? Two? Or may it be eternity? Love makes you do crazy things. Deep within I'm wondering, does he really love me? Love must have a hold on me. Mom told me when I was little, "You can't buy love." If anybody purchases it, let me know. I'm not asking for too much, but my head keeps telling me *"How long? How long?"*

The wait is over with, honey child. How long is finally here.

# The Ghosts of Yesterday
# Part 1

It seems just like yesterday that you both were still living. It seems like yesterday that you both had died. I would give anything just to hear your voices again.

I get so lonely at times. It seems like nobody understands me. I hear my inner voice in my head, trying to guide me. If only my subconscious mind would listen. I'm around so many people. Yet everybody likes giving orders and nobody follows them.

Can you tell me what I did that was so wrong? What am I being punished for? If I ever blew up and made a scolding face, if I made an awful comment under my breath, I'm sorry. Forgive me Papa, for I remember you whipped me and my brothers for playing in the fresh basket of laundry clothing.

You weren't aware of it. I thought about ten ways to get even with you. Payback is a real _itch. Now. I never tried to blow up and jump bad with you. The whole world would know about it. The other side would have been sooner for me, rather that later.

Papa, thank you for encouraging me to be all that I can be. You told me how you wished and dreamed that you had gotten your education. Thank you for never setting any limitations on us. I have fallen many times. I have cried many nights. I have laughed at many of the memories that we had. Papa, it was not the pain that brought me back to life. It was the will to survive. It was not how life beat me down, it was how I got back up. I didn't focus on the blows, but how I could stop them. I never tried to wallow in self-pity, for it weakened my strength.

You always told me that there are two kinds of fools. A regular fool and a store bought fool. A fool you can teach. A store-bought fool you will never be able to teach. Papa, that is why I'm using my mind rather than letting it use me. It's so hard at times. I will charge full speed ahead. I'm the captain and the co-pilot. Why should you let anyone else control your destiny if it is not God?

Mamma, thank you for your jokes and the harsh truth. I don't blame you for the things you didn't know. It is okay. I'll learn all I can for you. You were bright in your own ways.

What you have planted deep within my soul, a plastic surgeon would not be able to remove. Papa, anything that is absorbent I'm sucking in. The education you didn't get, let me get it for you. Just like you said, "take advantage of it." Every opportunity and chance that comes my way, I'll be sure to grab. Papa, if I missed it the first time, I will keep trying until I have it. I promise.

You are my ghosts of yesterday.

# What a Friend

The still wind will not roar
The still wind shall never roar
Twilight visions and sea quest dreams
Give me my enlightened wings so that I can soar
Soar back to our homeland
A place where our forefathers sighed
Glazing hot sun where the Moogi dance
How can I be so wrong?
Hold me, be there for me
Very soon I will be strong, I will be strong
Two worlds, similar in their own way
What I learn, forever with me will it stay
You have shown me the road
A road of adventure and humor too
In your mind forever, love your soul
It's the only thing that never grows old
Thanks for the truth and understanding
Together the future we were planning
Somehow, fate said no
Why do I have to let go?
No one knows but you and me
Just how we laughed under the full moon
While we hide beneath the jungle grass and count the stars in the sky
Moogi, I praise you
The present will remain true
Your water entered my land
United through life our friendship will expand
Our nation so gentle and delicate
You and I together, are you ready for the ride?

These few passages are dedicated to all the good friends both far and near. Some of us can describe in so many ways that there are no friends like old friends, they're like precious treasures embarked upon the sea, you love them and cherish them with morals and virtues, and then they immerse back into the sea. So remember the great times you shared with each other. How you played and held hands. It's truly a blessing to have such a wonderful person in your life.

# Early May

There comes a very delicate time in our lives when we think that love will endure forever and will never fade. Love can be a genie in a bottle, rub it the wrong way and he will escape, treat him poorly and he will wash away. I have a little story about a genie.
He was not mine, he was a gift. A loan for a split second before he vanished into the waves of the water, forever. Let's make a long story short; he was never mine. Now, when push comes to shove, I'm more than happy that I didn't choose him blocking up my sunshine.

# May

This is the day
The day I walk away
You were on my mind heavy, sweetheart
Hoping in my mind all over again, should we start?
I'm a young fool so in love
Cupid gave me a rough shove
If I walked away
Who would make you happy and gay?
I'm so bull-headed.
Harder than a steel needle being threaded
I tried to hide my true feelings
All I got was a short hand in my card dealing
Come back honey, come on back
Don't leave me hanging like a wet coat on a rack
Let me be the one to make your bed
No doubt about it, we will paint this town red
This is the day
The day indeed I walk away
I refuse to look back
Honey, this train jumped on some other tracks
I got to keep on trucking
A rotten relationship is what I'm ducking

# Star of Hope

You're my star of hope
Shining brightly on my rope
My every thought is of you
When I do the things I do
I don't want to be a fool
Spinning around on a stupid stool
I'd rather be a fool in love
Forever like a hand in a glove
I know you have been hurt
T he expression on your face still lurks
I think it's so unfair
When the one you love doesn't care
I haven't had a crook of a chance
Just a phone call and a very quick glance
Oh star of hope
Shining brightly on my rope
I see the hurt in your eyes
Don't worry, let me be your sunrise
Please keep me deep in your thoughts
Every little moment in your heart
I'll treat you better than gold
My love for you is coming from my soul
Is there a space in your mind I can hold?
Oh star of Hope
This loneliness won't let me cope
I'm neither mean nor cruel
I wish I were the woman who knew all of your love rules
Be the one and only in your life
A good lover and friend, not just another wife
I guess, Oh star of hope
You hold the key to be.

Open up your heart for me
Give me a try
Baby, view what the eyes can't see
You're my star of Hope
Forever shining brightly on my rope

# All Dogs Don't Have Tails

What?
All dogs don't have tails
If it walks like a dog
If it barks like a dog
Then doggone it
It is a dog
They don't discriminate
Some are females
They come in all colors and sizes.
If a dog says I love you
Should you believe it?
Rest assure a dog
Always has a second house
That is right
Don't blame me
For your mistrust
Don't blame me
For your insecurity
Your lies and devilish ways
Will catch you
And pile that nasty
Puppy food on your plate
The plate in which you
Push on someone else's table
Some of the old dogs
Are worth more than the young one
A dog wags it tail
Shiver below the knees
And lie like a dog
I was told every dog has their day
Well rest assure
Every puppy has their night.
It makes me laugh
When some people

Think they are larger that life
The same God that created you
Also made me too
Yes, rest assure you will
Get the prize that's coming to you
Trust me all dogs don't have tails

# Hang Not Thy Head

Hang not thy head in shame
God loves you just the same
Little black, African boy
Gripping that Holy Book as your toy
Go on, go on, God is on your side
Craving for knowledge and full of pride
Hang not they head in shame
Trotting the roads holding your dream instead
Hang not thy head in shame
Hang not thy head in shame
Who are you?
A great disciple or a Langston Hughes
Hang not thy head
Hold your dream instead
There is life around the bend
A change for a brother man to win
Lift thy head up very high
Like a dove until wisdom flies
Rise up above all nations
Love everyone without any allegation
Hang not thy head
Go in peace, instead
Hang not thy head
Never forgetting the motherland and the bloodshed
Strive to be the best
Each man will go through a test
A test of courage and strength
Who knows our days and length?
Hang not thy head
Keep grace in your heart instead

# Happy Mother's Day Mom

This is a gorgeous day of autumn. Mom, I'm sitting in my room recalling all your jokes and all the times you gave me a check yourself-card. I know you're gone from this earth-plane in the physical form but in the spiritual form I know you are always with me.

Thank you mom for tolerating all the good and not so good things I have done and how you endure all the not so pleasant cuts that life dealt you. Mom what a wonderful job you have accomplished. You are more than a super woman more precious than any diamond on the face of Africa

Mom I simply love you and your loving memory will never leave me. Thank you for being the woman that you were, for you have made me all that I am.

# Happy Mother's Day Mom

Happy Mother's Day mom
I remember how you held me in your arms
Happy Mother's Day mom
Thank you for all that you have done
Holding our hands and never letting go
Prudence and virtues are what I know
Fighting all of our large small battles
Picking me up when my heart get shattered
Happy Mother's Day mom
Thank you for keeping me from so much harm
Well mom now that you're not around
Sometimes my soul crumbles to the ground
I just remember the words you have said
Trying to keep a pure heart
Sometimes I forget to say my prayers before bed
Mom this one is for you
Only God knows what you have been through
I love you mom
You will always be in my heart
Forever in the Almighty's arm
Happy Mother's Day mom
I love you

# Protobe Black

Protobe black
The blacker the berry
Then the sweeter the juice
Protobe black
Is what I am
One hundred percent
In each and every gram
The complete package
Is what you see
Kinky hair
Dark skin
Sometimes nothing but white teeth
Protobe black
Almighty
Who can ever walk in my tracks?
To tell me you know
How to live my life
And what to do
Only God knows
The amount of hoops
I have to crawl through
Crawl walk and cry
Birth and life
Bills and more bills
Problems and pain
Pleasures and smiles
Struggle, hardship
A single parent
Show me
A good relationship
I might laugh
Perhaps even cry
Getting old
Then older

Then kick
The bucket
You just sit stand
Lay down and then die
Protobe black
Is what I am?
Protobe black
Who can ever walk?
In my track?
Nobody I must say
Protobe black
That's who I am

# The Bay

I heard chanting sounds
I stared and paused, no one was around
Could it be that I'm going crazy
Love can put you in a daisy
The whispering sound of love
Sweeter than a petal of a rose shrub
At the happy dock on the bay
I love my Nay
My sweet dear Nay
Our love will last forever
Wise, young but very clever
Overlooking the bay
I see myself in this glamorous gown one day
The water by the bay is very still
Go ahead, take him at your will
My dear Nay
How long will you stay?
I stood and cleared my head
Remembering those lovely words he said
I know that I really adore you
Our friendship shall remain true
The bay will not tell
Passion, memory forever will dwell
By the bay
My sweet pal, Nay.

# Simply Me

You're breaking my heart
In one million little pieces
The love mechanic had to
Give it a jump start
I still care for you
Even though
This situation is not new
Stop blaming me!
For the entire thing that didn't go right
Wash, and burn, and throw that stuff out of sight
Don't compare me with someone else
She has her own mind
Guess what
I'm myself
Let me be me
I like a lover who
Laughs, cries, and takes long walks
Not just lips who constantly talk. I'm only human
All I know is that
I care for you
You said what goes around comes around
Right now, your words are knocking me down
I refuse to go there
No matter how many times
You have been hurt
Just don't judge me
With those other man-eating ladies
Who strive for nothing but hurt
Clever laughter and money eaters
I'm a romantic sweet young thing
Not a disturbed, wild, man-beater

I'm the queen of all hearts
No other woman can fill my part
This love is so fast
Will it give me a second try?
Come on, stop this craziness
Don't let love pass you by

# Still Water

Wade the water of still movement.
Wade the waters
I took a walk through the field of still waters
I heard echoes of the past
It was the past of yesterday's ghost
The beloved one of so many
Old still waters have washed them
Whiter than snow
Still waters have made them new again
The only thing that will run on and on
It's the road of still water
Water in which brought us here
The road of water that will one day
Carry us all away
I tried to speak to the still waters
They didn't reply back
I used to wake up everyday
Cry, laugh, and not think about my friend in still water
Time is so precious
Grasped by the hands of the Almighty
An appointment that is set by Him
A time in which man came into this cold, bittersweet world
Traveling through time, matter and space
Hitting all the pitfalls that trap the soul for life
Old still water is always still
Still waters are a reservoir
A time linked to destiny
A time judged by the stars and moon
An honor given by the Almighty God
What is so still about it?
The one whom I use to love is wading the waters of peace
Sleeping in the spiritual plane
Old still water, wash their hearts clean
Old still water, revive their soul

Old still water, thy judgment waits short of thy coming.
Young soul, old one, who has gone on
The limb of time will always stand on the banks
Still waters
Forever and ever
In God, the Almighty, will I pray
Until thy still waters wash my ashes away

# Old Mighty Pen

Give me a pen
I will be fine
I have the power to change the speed of time
I'm going to tell you a little story
Everything is not sugarcoated and on the road to glory
I'm writing about this old world today
Please listen to every word I have to say
Racism, vandalism, high taxes, and rent
Presidents, doctors, and lawyers who give a red cent
Give me my pen
I'll tell everything up and down, out and in
Why was I back in this old place?
An unstable environment with no smiling faces
My pen will tell it all
From the streets to the steps of city hall
If you know the elite you're fine.
If you do not
Then you're just another sad soul lost in time
This city can be harsh and cold
I want my share of the gold
I want my time and space
A huge house and a swimming pool
Straight in the woods one less face
Give me my pen
I will set the record straight
This old cycle I have to break

# Flash Back

I saw my whole young life flash by
If I had to start over again I wouldn't try
So hard, I found myself very dumb
Chasing love like a child after bubble gum
Expressing myself like a high priestess
Calling, looking from the North and East
A straight-out fool
Young and crazy, high upon an uncivilized stool
Mamma said, you couldn't buy love
Yet so many people try hard to
Until their heart turns blue
Oh what a crazy fool I have been
Girl, I got to put this trash to and end
I refuse to run behind a man
Most of them are short on sense and don't understand
Finally I meet one with a sense of humor and knowledge
Smart and cute and loaded on the wallet
All I know is I like him a lot
Very skeptical if he played ball in my court
Perhaps he would brag and shoot the shots
He probably tells everything that he knows
I really don't have time for a freak show
Sometimes the past hides the flaws
Broken hearts and hurting eyes will never forget what they saw
Flash back, going back into time
Flashing heavy over again on my little mind

# The Unknown

Why do so many people fear the Unknown?
I can see the hidden things revealed and shown
Concentrate, concentrate, and meditate
The Divine Law is always straight
It's really the Unknown
The Almighty God, high on his throne
Give praise to Him at your own pace
Let not your heart go to waste
Dark, darker than dark or night
Let your spiritual guide be your light
The Unknown is our ancestor's original way
The old African method on how to pray
Concentration and meditation; that is the way
To us, our path will be shown
A word of wisdom from the Unknown

# Black History

Up from a trail of hard work
Chains and scars mark the hurt
A trail of nothing but pure hate
A trail long overdue, far too late
A trail of blood
No justice, no love
It was just an ego and skin thing
Try virtues and morals, see what that brings?
Divided by a lack of understanding
Divided by a lack of common sense
The fog of liberty is still a little dense
Some people do not know that the Almighty is above all nations
Treating one another right is just half of the equation
If God loves everybody and everything, then so can we
We got to start living in harmony
There is only one judge and His truth shall prevail
Stop this sin; I'm better than you are, trail
We are free but not at last
Look to the future and never forget the rocky past
Somewhere the trail of slavery still cooks on
I can stop this trail; I feel the power in my bones
If all races unite, hatred will shrink and will be all alone
Ride with peace and sing a brand new song
The mountaintop will be standing there
I can feel hope riding on a wing and a prayer
The ghost of yesterday has faded away
In a vision of dreams I saw a better day
It's a moral that will endure to the end of time
Run on my friend, the road is near
A bell of freedom is what I hear
Justice for you and me, justice for all
All backgrounds, green, brown, big and small

# Strings from the Past

Do not tie me down
With the strings
From the past
For I do not
Want to sit
In the seat
Of anger
I do not want
To drink from
The cup of bitterness
I will not ride
The waves of hate
I have come much
Much too far
To look back now
My eyes are locked
On the present
For the past is
What it is said to be?
The past
Do not tie me
Nor bind me
With old rivals
I care not to know
About them
Nor what hand in life
Has the wheel turned for them
Tie me not with
The strings from the past
My soul is humble
My mind is free
And my spirit is clean
I cannot change it
I'm living for today

And thinking about what
Tomorrow may bring
Tie me not with
The strings from the past
It is gone
Rolled away with time
I wish not to pull it back
Please do not tie me with
The strings from the past

# Black or White Love

Would you love me if I were white?
Would you love me if I were black?
Love shows strong emotions
Ask God
He always knows
What if my hair was hard and kinky, skin darker than a berry?
What if my hair was blonde and my eyes light blue?
Would you still love me?
Although I am not as smart as you are
Maybe my parents do not love me like yours do
They cannot stop this rendezvous
So what if I am white?
So what if I am black?
Neither mountain nor sea will keep us apart
White love or black, that is for me to decide
Never, never tell me I am not good for a white man
Nor should I not be in love with one
Black love is so fine that money cannot buy it
You should love me even if I were blacker than
Midnight, eyes redder than fire
Black love or white
Take a step deeper and look within, my friend
God created men and women for love, not for skin color
May God bless you and keep you in the presence of His power
That is what white or black love should be about

# Black Cat

I'm worse than a black cat
I have more than nine lives
Just don't quote me on that
I have been through fire and pain
Black cat is surely my nickname
My back doesn't consist of bones.
Only thorns and cement stones
I have walked many paths all alone.
Rejection and unhappiness
Will no direction to home
This Old World
Can be a very cold place
No true friends who remember your face
My life still extends on
Just when I think it is over
I pop back ten times as strong
I'm going to hold my head up
Keep on and thrive
I know I got more than nine lives
Black cat just as bad as can be
There will never be another after me

# Merry Christmas Mom and Dad

It has been so long since
I heard your voices
A big, scented pine tree
A clear, cold sky smiling down at me
Neighbors all around cheerful as can be
Our old house stuffed with memories
The two families bless each one of us
Forever in God will our souls trust
Believing in God, yes we must
Everybody snuggled tight, in his or her bed
I'm too old to imagine a big belly Santa in red
Merry Christmas Mom and Dad
Your corn bread stuffing and potato pie
In the dreams I imagined I had
It has been a very long time
Thousands of miles from home you are still on my mind
No more children, they are all grown
Far away in Boston, three still at home
Merry Christmas Mom and Dad
This year is rolling in; I'm feeling empty and sad
You were the best thing I ever had
One for the Present
One for the Future, and two for the Past
Merry Christmas Mom and Dad

# Old Timer

It was a calm and clear fall evening when the chilling words of my father's ghost whispered to me as though the echo was sitting in my college classroom. A ghost that tried to guide me and keep me on the right path. The ghost that is dead but truly in spirit, he still lives on. I was told that a parent could hold their child's hand for a little while, but forever hold their heart. I totally agree, as the fruit that comes from the vine, and water flows from the nature, earth as moon, light to the night, and sun to day, one can't exist without the other. In each little sense, they are all connected and will always remain joined together.

Pop, if you are looking down and can see me, I'm writing this one for you, and in my heart you will always live and in my soul you will stay.

# Old Timer

Born so long ago
Wisdom, understanding is what I know
Load up the horse and the mule
Pull pick and dig that is the rule
I'm just passing through
I will leave this body
And journey somewhere new
I'm not here for long
I love you
I will never tell you anything wrong
Old Timer, old but very wise
My gray hair these dreary eyes
I wont be here too long
Going down the Nile
To another home

So long, so long, so long
You are gone but
Your spirit lives on
Thanks Old Timer
For the gratitude you have shown

In loving memory of my father, rest on old timer



Forever A Temptation

I wrote "Forever A Temptation" because of the chilling effect that the people and the movie had upon me. I grew up listening to their music and my mother telling me about them, as if she knew them personally. As I sit in my room and watch the movie for two days straight, the first day was pumping with hope and gave me the power to conquer all of my dreams. The second day was fine until the part came on about Melvin. I couldn't hold back the hurt I felt inside and words can never describe it.

A mountain of tears came streaming down my young but innocent face as though the world around me wouldn't be around anymore, as my soul sank deeply into the ground.

One of the best times and the first times I have ever gone to a live concert was July 15, 1999. I prayed to God that the weather would not alter the concert's original date. Yes, I would get a chance to see the real thing being put into action, the real deal, the Temptations. What a great thrill I got when I picked up the ticket at the box office theater. I was smiling and day dreaming like a Cheshire cat from ear to ear.

Otis William, I wrote this one for you. I tired hard to get in backstage and didn't succeed. Otis, next time I will not have this problem at all.

# Forever A Temptation

No matter what forever a temp
Your style and rhyme
No one can crimp
**Melvin** your lovely baritone voice
If I picked a lover
You would be my choice
My dear friends
Paul and Eddie
**Southern boys at a fast pace**
**Were you ready?**
He was always heard
**And had to be seen**
Bold **David** with his rainbow dreams
Deep within I know what feel
**Otis** teaching them black love is real
Temps where did you go wrong?
Life fame and death you move on
Forever a temp
**Otis** his sensational love
It will never be crimp
Forever you will be a Temptation

# The Learning Tree

I'm a human being
Striving in this imperfect world
Don't put your trust in me
I'm learning from the wisdom tree
I went out to pick understanding
I tried to borrow knowledge
A floating spirit in a human form
Stationed on the earth-plane
Just a huge college dorm
I'm prone to make errors
Almighty, give me strength
As I climb this hill of perils
If I had wings, I would fly away
A peaceful place I would stay
I'm a human being
Living in an imperfect world
There are so many changes around you
Nothing is the way it used to be
Child molesters, murderers, and crooks
Liars, call girls, and pimps
Everybody wants to shout hallelujah on Sunday
If God strikes with His mighty hand today
How many of us are living by the Holy Book?
I'm learning from the tree of knowledge
Located on the earth-plane
One huge college
Judge me not
Point not your finger at me
Get ready for your beating

When you reach your punishment tree
Oh father universe and mother earth
I'll accept knowledge, understanding, and wisdom
From the learning tree
Until ashes again
From this day forward so may it be

# Drama Queen

Waiting to cause a big scene
A downright natural drama queen
Standing on the front porch
While she lights up a cancer torch
Head rag mamma
Minute by minute waiting for drama
Chasing the mailman down
For your welfare check
Shopping, cigarette, and rent you can bet
More broke than a glass vase in a week
This same old ritual you repeat
Change your life drama queen
One hundred miles per hour
On the telephone talking a lot of crap
It's time for your nap
Hit a book, enroll in college
You can get a boat-load of understanding and knowledge
Drama queen, please
Your welfare is running out
Job training, college registration, and expensive childcare
Headaches, midterms, and stress there's no doubt
Stop causing a putrid scene
Change your attitude and life, miss drama queen.

# Lover's Hands Part 2

The hands turned ugly. We no longer love each other. We use words of hate. Love has faded away. I can feel it deep in my bones, as if someone else controlled your very soul. My lover used his hurting hands. He used his insulting words. Raging demons caused him to strike me. I can care less if he leaves and never returns. I don't care if he goes to the end of the world, at least hurt and pain can't find me.

Go away, go away. This is not what love is supposed to be. I expected rainbow dreams and four-leaf clovers. Blue and black marks are on my face now. Scars that a plastic surgeon could never remove are the marks in which my lover put there. Lover, what have you done? A bag of raging lies have destroyed our love for each other. Did someone put an evil and wicked curse upon us? This wasn't meant to be. You were the most adorable thing I had ever seen. You were the apple of my eyes, the wind beneath my wings, and the sunshine of the day. I'm under new management. I want my maiden name back. I want all of my love back. I want everything I had given you back, including my time. Go away, bad days. I wish that time would roll away, the minutes, and hours wouldn't be anymore. I wish you were no more.

Expectations are not always what they seem. They're sometimes a let down, a down fall in all of our expectations. A drop in all of our dreams. Never put your eggs in one basket; never forget to count your blessings. Always give thanks to God the Almighty. Always be very grateful. Expectations are like dreams or hope; they don't always become reality, they shatter like fragile glass, and they run away like a thief in the night. They roll away like the hungry sea searching for love, when no love is to be found.

# The Ghosts of one Silk Stocking
# Part 1

Sit right on down, and enjoy this crawling creepy short story about a spook who is in love with a silk stocking.

A beautiful fall day in a quite little town of Hollowly New Jersey. A very lovely couple was trying to find a comfortable cozy and safe place. Jeff and his wife Cindy of fifteen years along with their two children. Ryan age eleven and Melissa age fourteen. Who just got the surprising, and best news they had heard all day. Their real state agent Linda Scareaway had just called to say, they were approved for the five bedroom cottage three bath 3,899 square feet house had been approved. This warm and cozy house is near this little town called Hollowly located in New Jersey. Can you image the glow on Linda and Jeffery faces. It was a warm and sunny day in Hollowly. When Linda and Jeffery walk into the real-estate office to sign the final paperwork for their house

On September the 13, 1988. Linda and Jeffery and their two child Melissa and Ryan pulled up into the driveway and started to unload all of there furniture of the bright yellow Rider truck. Jeffrey stood about 6 feet tall and was very stocky around two hundred pounds with strawberry hair. And sparkling gray eyes. Linda a little petite lady with blue eyes and the golden skin of the ripe and mouth-watering olive, with shoulder length blonde hair. As Melissa and Ryan heart pounded with thrill to see the door swing wide open to there new house. Jeffrey turns the key to open the door of their new house located at 616 Hollowly Drive. As Jeffrey stepped inside the house the fresh scent of new paint greeted them. The sound of musical chimes swings back and forward as the autumn wind blew gently. Jeffery view upstairs first and then headed downstairs. The kitchen was ivory with hunter green and very huge with three Australia chandelier suspending from the ceiling. The three and a half baths were periwinkle with ivory floors. The fireplace was built out of granite marble on each side imported from Swissiland and the stone around the cozy warm fireplace was imported from the mountains of Denver. The bedrooms with painted baby blue trim with eggshell white.

# Sit Back and Watch

There's no need
To get revenge
Revenge's the boggie man
Some people
Let the boggie man
Completely fuck them up
All that hate
Malice
Vemous talk
Gossip
Spreading lies and rumors like mayo
Hoo-Doo
Voo-Doo
What go around
Come back around
Ten times folded
Some things
Was menat to be
It is
Wat it's
But in your mind
You're to blind to see
Everything has a purpose
Wheter we
Like it or not
Sometimes
It 'll hurt
Hit
Bite
Knock you out
Before it
Knock
Bite

Hit or
Hurt me
The boggie man is waiting for you
Thnik twice
Move three times
Turn of the lights
It's your call
You have a choice
To make things right